Exploring the Latin American Mind

Exploring The Latin American Mind

Seymour B. Liebman

Nelson-Hall nh Chicago

Other books by this author:
The Enlightened: The Writings of Luis de Carvajal, el Mozo
      with Preface by Alan Nevas
The Jews in New Spain
The Great Auto de Fe of 1649 in Mexico
The Inquisitors and the Jews in the New World
The Middle East: A Return to Facts

Library of Congress Cataloging in Publication Data

Liebman, Seymour B   1907-
    Exploring the Latin American mind.

    Bibliography: p.
    Includes index.
    1.   Latin America—Civilization.   2.   National
characteristics, Latin American.   I.   Title.
F1408.3.L5   980   76-6847
ISBN 0-88229-134-3

Contents

Preface   vii

1   Myths, Illusions, and Insights   1

2   Geography and Language   16

3   The Latin American Search for Identity   34

4   Machismo and Sex   49

5   Religion   60

6   The Family   79

7   The Middle Class   90

8   Anti-Hispanism — the Indian   104

9   Citizenship, Government, and Revolutions   113

10 Universities, Schools, and Students   126

11 Nationalism, Xenophobia, and Chauvinism   144

12 Latin America and the United States   165

Bibliography   183

Index   189

11779

Preface

When I first arrived in Mexico and began a study of Latin America, I came across three statements that I since have had reason to recall. The first was that if one wanted to write about Mexico, one should stay there only thirty days. If one stayed for sixty, doubts about the accuracy of one's observations would arise, and after ninety days, the task of interpreting the many conflicting aspects of the people and the culture would become almost impossible. The second statement was made by ex-Senator Gruening of Alaska in his book, *Mexico and Its Heritage*, first published in 1928. He wrote that anything that one said about Mexico was true and could be corroborated. The third statement declared that the history of Mexico is legend with footnotes.

Although my wife and I lived in Mexico for more than six years and traveled extensively throughout Latin America for over eleven years, it was not until we had returned to the United States and lived here for three years that sufficient objectivity and perspective were achieved.

It would be unusual for anyone who reads this book and

who regards himself as an authority on Latin America (especially two- or three-week tourists) to agree with all that it contains. Gruening's statement is still true! So is the third statement.

The real story of Latin America, its people, its fascinating and dramatic history, has yet to be written. Too many books are written for special purposes of the Department of State, the Central Intelligence Agency (CIA), by pro-Church advocates or anti-Church interests, or other propagandists, not to mention tourist bureaus of governments or travel agencies.

The few good texts usually deal with dates and events and simplistic interpretations. They are almost devoid of interpretations of value systems, psychological, sociological, and anthropological aspects of the cultures of the Latin American nations. The best books are those written by the anthropologists, to which must be added the works of the economic historian, Frank Tannenbaum.

John Gerassi, journalist and author, accuses the Associated Press and the United Press International of being "completely unreliable in Latin America" (18:43).* He levels the charge of misrepresenting the facts on Latin America to our entire press (18:47). One need not mention that the estimable *New York Times* is partially responsible for the ridiculous misunderstanding of Fidel Castro prior to 1960.

Many tourists spend a short holiday in Latin America—twelve days in twenty countries, or vice versa—and are frequently the naive victims of imaginative tourist guides. Others observe strange customs, and, without any background, dispense opinions about the culture and people they saw fleetingly and out of historical context. An obstacle to empathic understanding of other cultures is the formation of value judgments based upon one's own cultural experiences. Such comparisons, or judgments, are frequently the basis

---

*References are to the appended bibliography. The first number is that of the book and second is the page number.

of misunderstanding and the cause of compounded errors.

Patterns of culture result from historical origins and experience, economic structures, religious and ethical values, and a host of other influencing factors. The definition of cultural anthropology, "learned behavior socially transmitted," is apt. Since our own cultural experiences are so vastly different from those in Latin American countries, we need to seek information from qualified sources rather than from travel posters, brochures, propaganda, and slogans.

It is ironic that in a time when the means of communication—printed, oral and pictorial—are easily accessible to almost all people we should so largely rely upon slogans and labels to convey ideas and mental images. The acceptance of slogans and labels stultifies thinking and encourages vague generalizations. Labels are usually invented by those who are more interested in gaining emotional acceptance for their ideas or concepts than in imparting factual information or motivating thinking.

We have been mesmerized and assaulted by such soporific titles as "New Deal," "Fair Deal," and "New Frontier." More recently we were asked to salute the banner of "The New Federalism." We were expected to shout hosannas for the Marshall Plan (it was good), the Alliance for Progress (may it rest in peace, which is a better fate than it deserves), and now, "Trade Not Aid." Slogans are not adequate substitutes for an understanding of needs and problems or for intelligent plans to solve them.

Advocates of the teaching of Spanish in the elementary schools preach that such bilingualism is the panacea for improving understanding of Latin America and our relationships with it. Such theorizing is as fallacious as the use of slogans to improve thinking. It is indisputable that knowing the language of a foreign country with which one is to deal, or which one is to visit, has certain advantages. But the knowledge of the language is far from a guarantee that meaningful communication can take place between peoples or governments. Knowing words is not synonymous with attitudes and values of a people. It is upon knowledge of the latter that any meaningful communication must be based. Also each language has nuances and idioms that cannot be taught in school. The following illustrates how misunderstandings can arise from a single word.

When General Victoriano Huerta took over the presidency of Mexico in 1913 after the assassination of President Francisco Madero, President Woodrow Wilson insisted that Mexico hold popular elections. Huerta advised Wilson that they would be held *proximo*. The Spanish word is not a cognate of the English "proximate." *Proximo* does not mean "immediately," or "very soon," or "next month," which are the definitions in English dictionaries. In Spanish, *proximo* means "soon" or "sometime in the future." When several months passed without a scheduling of public elections, Wilson determined to enforce his interpretation of what he thought Huerta had promised him. He sent the United States Navy into the Mexican port of Veracruz. This incident is one which is still resented by some Mexican and other Latin American politicians.

Despite good intentions, United States political and economic policies based upon superficial and myopic understanding of underlying problems resulted in short range enthusiasm and long range failure. In addition to witnessing the debacle of grandiose plans, we have frequently earned the enmity of those we tried to aid. Fundamentally, North Americans are unaware of the values, aspirations, patterns of behavior, and character of the Latins. Understandings in these areas are the conduits to better relationships. The writer of this book recognizes the magnitude of the task of bringing such understandings to readers, and concedes that this opus is something less than a definitive work.

In an approach to acquiring understandings of other peoples, Americans are handicapped by their tendency to oversimplify. The desire, or need, for oversimplification leads to conceptualizations in terms of general models or patterns which are familiar to Americans. Naturally, we think as

Americans, act as Americans, and relate all problems to the patterns and formulae which we pursue in our own lives and which bear the stamp, "Made in America." We also make verbal obeisance to the Golden Rule, "Do unto others as you would have others do unto you." Harry Overstreet, in his book, *The Mature Mind,* wrote that empathy should replace the Golden Rule. He proposed a new rule, "Do unto others as they would choose to have you do unto them."

In our relationships with peoples of other cultures, it is essential that we first learn how they think, what their value system is, and what their goals and aspirations are. If there is any contribution that we, as Americans, can and should make, provided that a contribution other than dollars has been requested, then we should proceed and operate within the patterns and mores of the recipients.

We must add a comment on another overrated adjunct to the means of learning about other peoples—travel. Thomas Fuller said in 1737, "Travel makes a wise man better, but a fool worse." Travel and knowledge of the foreign language can accomplish much only if combined with empathy, knowledge of the culture (culture used in its anthropological sense), and a learning attitude.

Most things, or aspects of life, are in the greys, rather than being black or white. This is likewise true in discussions of cultures. If there are in this book any criticisms, implicit or implied, of any peoples, or governments, it is intended only that they serve to clarify the perspective. However, no observer is infallible, nor does each observer of any thing or people necessarily agree with others. My deep affection for the Latin Americans and the hope of adding to stronger bonds of friendship and understanding motivated the writing of this book. I trust that understandings to be acquired may serve as a bridge between all the peoples of the Western Hemisphere.

1 ● Myths, Illusions, and Insights

The two countries closest to our southern border are Cuba and Mexico. The first is separated from us by a narrow body of water, and the other is contiguous and shares a 1500-mile border with us. Floridians have a tendency to equate Cuba with all of Latin America, and Miamians refer to their airport as "The Gateway to Latin America."

Residents of the Southwest of the United States likewise regard their border towns—El Paso, Laredo, San Diego—as gateways to Latin America. However, in the main, Miami is used by Cubans and some Colombians and Mexicans as a port of entry. While Cuba and Mexico are both part of Latin America, Mexico is more representative of Latin America than is Cuba.

Cuba's closest Latin American neighbor is Mexico. The propinquity has not resulted in any noticeable acculturation by either. The greatest figures of each of these countries fled to the United States when they had to seek refuge. Hidalgo, Juarez and Madero of Mexico, and José Marti, the Apostle of Cuba, came to these shores when their lives were endangered.

No Cuban fled to Mexico in the 1890s, nor did Mexico aid Cuba to secure its independence from Spain, which occurred with the aid of America, the land of the gringo.

It is interesting to note that the word *gringo* used to be a pejorative and was applied primarily to Americans. It is still in use, but it is now applied to almost all foreigners and has lost much of the opprobrium that it formerly possessed. Edwin B. William's *Spanish-English Dictionary* (1971 edition) defines *gringo* as "a foreigner." One of the fanciful explanations for the derivation of the word is that General "Black Jack" Pershing's troops, who "invaded" Mexico in 1916 in an attempt to catch Pancho Villa, used to sing a song, "Green Grow the Lilacs," and Mexican natives created the word *gringo* from the first two words. This naive philology, however, must be discarded since the Argentinian poet, José Hernandez, has a line in his epic poem, "Martin Fierro," "Era un gringo tan bozal!" The poem was written in 1872, almost a half century before Pershing's futile expedition.

The word *bozal* was usually applied in South America to Negroes recently brought from Africa, or one who did not speak Spanish well or correctly. This definition was applied to the word *negro* in Guatemala and Mexico. A Negro who could understand Spanish and could speak it understandably was a *negro ladino*. We shall see that *ladino* had other meanings.

While many Habaneros (residents of Havana) and residents of Mexican border towns incorporated English words into their language, the resulting vocabularies have different names. In Mexico, the bastardized language is called *pocho,* a slang term meaning also "rotten" or "a lie." In Havana, the language mixture is known as *barbarismo.* The use of the native tongue, Spanish, its vocabulary and pronunciation, is different in the two countries. These differences might be shrugged off as being inconsequential, but these differences in close Latin American neighbors are symbolic of the fact that there are thousands of things that differentiate the countries of Latin America. Ignorance of such differences has caused and still continues to cause problems among all of the nations of the Western Hemisphere.

There is a serious misconception about the very entity of the area that we call Latin America. The basic misconception consists of regarding Latin America as a continental homogeneous community of shared interests, having a sense of mutual responsibility and sharing a common heritage.

It has been said that Latin America (excluding Argentina and Brazil) is the heir of two cultures—Indian and Spanish. Even if this were true and one disregarded the other cultural influences, the exceptions would confirm the fact that Latin American states are not homogeneous. Furthermore, there is no single Spanish or Indian culture. There are hundreds of Indian cultures and the differences among them permeate almost every phase of life. There has been no complete fusion of Spanish culture with any one Indian culture. Many illustrations advanced by pro-fusionists do not take into account the great dissimilarities found in the Indian cultures that existed prior to the arrival of the Spaniards in the New World. We have found no proof that the Indians of Mesoamerica were even aware of the existence of the Indians in South America or the Caribbean area.

George Santayana wrote many years ago in his book, *Character and Opinion in the United States*, "Comparison is the expedient of those who cannot reach the heart of the things compared." Since Santayana himself pleaded guilty to resorting, at times, to making comparisons, so, in some rare instances, comparisons will be utilized in this book to make comprehensible what might otherwise be difficult to comprehend by the uninitiated.

The Spanish literary giant and historian, Ramón Menéndez Pidal, said that austerity is the "basic quality of the Spanish character." Don Ramón also noted that the Spaniard gives no heed to the morrow, meeting each difficulty as it presents itself. These same characteristics are consistently attributed to the Indians. The exceptional Incas of Peru were great planners. For instance, they built storehouses for surplus grains in the event of a drought in later years. The Spaniard, as well as the Indian, lacks curiosity about foreign cultures, and both are highly indifferent to pure science. Trogus Pompeius observed, almost 2000 years ago, that the Iberian psyche is as well prepared for death as their bodies are for abstinence and toil. These characteristics also apply to the Indians. Just as the Spaniard sacrificed his life in loyalty to his lord, so did the Indian permit himself to be sacrificed by his priests so that his blood could serve as food for his gods.

The foregoing and other similarities greatly facilitated the conquest of the Indian in Mesoamerica. The similarities gave a superficial appearance of acceptance of the Spanish religion and mores, but the differences, or variances, in character and psyche were greater than the likenesses. We shall see in the chapter on "The Indian" that there are over 250 Indian cultures. When subjected to the Spanish sword and the proselytization of the monks, most Indians merely made expedient adjustments and remained untouched, unassimilated, and unintegrated into the new stream of life imported into their domains. The similarities have not been sufficient to weld Latin America into a homogeneous unit. Charles Wagley, a renowned social scientist, lived in Latin America and studied the people. He wrote that "the concept of a Latin America exists only in the United States where Latin American studies are pursued" (68:9).

Many perceptive remarks are made by Felipe Herrera in his essay "Disunity as an Obstacle to Progress." He summarizes the issues as follows:

> Moreover, the community of language, religion, institutions, law and authority [in Latin America] went no more than skin-deep, and this was the origin of the superposition of the appearance on reality—of the "apparent" nation on the "real" nation—that characterized almost the whole of Latin America until very late in the nineteenth century, and that still persists in some countries. . .the cultural patterns introduced and officially adopted by the Iberian immigrants made no attempt to blend with the geographic and economic reality to which they were applied. Thus, just as different

parts of the colonies were geographically isolated from one another, the alien culture was isolated from the indigenous culture because it was superimposed on it and was not integrated with it. [65:232] The new nations were even more isolated from one another than in their colonial past. [65:236] Integration among the Latin American nations has become a need for the future rather than an imperative of the past.[65:243]

There are too many who see all the peoples of south of the border sharing common interests, a common language, and a common faith (Catholic), and they regard the national boundaries of the various countries as almost artificial divisions.

If all things erroneously believed to be shared in common represented reality, then the perplexities and conundrums that beset solutions to problems of commercial unions, area cooperation, and joint attacks on similar economic and agrarian difficulties that bedevil so many of these nations would not exist. The peoples of these nations have little awareness of any close identity and affiliation with each other and possess little knowledge of one another. *Siempre,* a Mexican magazine, conducted a survey in 1965 of the amount of knowledge of other Latin American countries possessed by Mexicans in urban areas. The amount of ignorance revealed was devastating. Ecuadorians, Peruvians and Colombians not only are ignorant about other Latin Americans but also know little of their own compatriots in other parts of their country.

The stark reality that confronts almost all these nations is that they are attempting to catapult from a semi-feudal, stratified, non-literate society to a technological industrial society without the creation of mobility of status, and with inadequate and ill-programmed universities and educational systems plus inefficient, corrupt political systems. There is the failure to see the relationships between ways and means and the absence of any thought of changing the value system and establishing long-range goals.

The impediments to the realization of any of the

foregoing—much less the total—are factors that are not considered when modernization in Latin America is contemplated. The first of the impediments is that historical roots are not considered as an influence on the consideration of contemporary problems and their solutions. Historical roots and traditional mores are often stumbling blocks to proposed changes. Many Latins believe that all problems can be solved by money—begged, borrowed or stolen—or by nationalization of foreign-owned enterprises.

"Spend, spend, spend" appears to be the motto of politicians of all countries and "let future generations worry about repayment." If the future generations cannot find the funds, then let the creditors worry.

The second impediment has been termed "the functional equilibrium fallacy" by Wilbert E. Moore of Princeton University. He postulates that societies are viewed as "normally existing in a steady state of balanced and interdependent actions and forces, exceptionally and temporarily disrupted by the intrusive influence of eonomic and related changes" (12:2). He also notes that the "perceived differences among societies have been understated" (12:2). Professor Moore further observes that the two fallacies are closely related. The functional equilibrium fallacy causes minimizing of attention to long-term, gradual, and continuous change.

The facts are that (1) features of the past are always relevant to the present and historical heritage persists in some form even in post-revolutionary regimes; (2) general world history also bears on the differentiation in societies; and (3) from the legacies of the past of each nation and from the trajectory of its modernization, different tensions arise in the various countries and societies, and the management of these tensions will also vary.

Our government, as evidenced by the actions of its official branches and its unofficial extensions, appears to labor under the fallacies noted above while ignoring the facts. We play out the role of a salesman who seems obsessed by the need to get rid of his wares. We are persistent to the point of embarrassment in our determination to sell our ideas of democracy and freedom, our materialism, the obsolescence built into our manufactured products, and other tawdry aspects of our value system. We break down customer resistance through offering "give-aways" and "specials." We are not concerned with the customer's needs or his motivations in becoming a party to the deal or his ability to pay. The lack of utility of the product to the customer and the possible impracticality or inappropriateness of the item to the time or place seem of less than primary concern. We seek to duplicate our institutions and concepts and to re-create the world in our image. We are apparently ignorant of, or unconcerned with, the fact that the mores, value systems, and aspirations of one people cannot be transferred by contract or governmental fiat to others.

Mariano Picon Salas, a Venezuelan, declared that Latin Americans "cannot cut the umbilical cord linking our history to the sixteenth century Hispanic World" (49:37). The persistence of bonds to the past has created what Charles Wagley termed the "ideal pattern," which he defines as the "consensus of opinion as to how people should behave in particular situations" (68:2). These ideal patterns provide a "barrier to economic development, educational reform, and political modernization" (68:7).

José Ignacio Rasco wrote in 1968 that the "failure of past integrationist efforts may have resulted from a premature politization of certain ideological cultural trends or movements, in an excessively politically backward and disunited continent. . ." (*Americas*—publication of the Pan-American Union).

Colombia was the showcase for the Alliance for Progress and A.I.D. until 1964. Colombia is practically bankrupt despite the millions poured into it. During the years of the Alliance for Progress, a civil war raged in Colombia that had begun in 1948. The estimates of the number of Colombians killed by their own countrymen range from 250,000 to 500,000 and the slaughter has not come to a complete halt. The streets of Bogotá are now dirty, sidewalks broken and hazardous. Smuggled goods are sold openly on Avénida Séptima, the city's principal thoroughfare, and in Santa Marta right on the walk along the beach. Customs inspectors examine all cargo and packages as passengers disembark on intranational flights. The passing of bribes is open.

Under date of March 7, 1971, the Associated Press reported from Bogotá that "land-hungry Colombian peasants, copying their Chilean counterparts, have seized hundreds of farms. . . ." In Chile, over 300 illegal occupations of farms took place during the first year and a half of President Allende's regime. The occupations were organized by Marxist groups. There is some evidence that the Colombian peasants were inspired by Marxist disciples trained in Cuba or Chile. Carlos Villamil, former director of the Colombian agrarian agency, stated, "to make revolution in Colombia, it is not necessary to import agitators." The ELN (National Liberation Army), a guerilla movement, attacked and killed two Colombian policemen in February 1975.

Colombia has many "sister-cities" linked to Miami, Coral Gables and other Dade County, Florida, municipalities. What is the influence of this "sister city" relationship on the Colombian populace? What value is there in people-to-people programs except for publicity for city officials of both countries and for official junkets at the expense of the taxpayers? I can unequivocally state that I have failed to find people in any city in Latin America who have changed from anti-American to pro-American as a result of the two foregoing programs.

Rojas Pinilla was dictator and conducted a ruthless regime in Colombia, 1953–1957. He came to power by revolution and was removed by revolution. He was sentenced to jail for defalcations and raids on the public treasury. In the election of 1970, he came within a hair's breadth of winning the presidency in a popular election although he was opposed by a candidate supported by the two major parties who also had the blessings of the outgoing president, Carlos Lleras Restrepo. Lleras Restrepo's Liberal party is now split by warring factions as is the Conservative party. Rojas Pinilla, his daughter, Maria, and some labor leaders formed a third party, ANAPO, which has already drawn many from the other two parties. (Rojas Pinilla died in 1974.)

Forty-eight universities in Colombia were closed for periods ranging from forty-five days to six months during the year 1971. Although the new president Pastrana and most of his new ministers are honest and well-meaning, they are not politicos! A *politico* in Latin America is sophisticated, suave, ruthless when necessary. He lines his pockets and lets his followers line theirs. His speeches and promises serve as surrogates for action.

In this era of journalistic reporting and radio and television dissemination of fashions, foods and fads, there is an international common denominator in these areas. People in cosmopolitan areas look more alike than different. This fosters the illusion for tourists and hurried, if not harried, observers that the similarities are more basic than they actually are. Basic values and mores are only superficially influenced by skirt lengths and Coca Cola. The confluence of attitudes, values, and self-concepts, aspirations, perceptions and abilities which motivate Latin Americans have their origins in their unique, old, and rich multiheritage. Understanding Latin American people requires an understanding of their historical heritage.

Latin Americans who are proud of their white, or European, or Caucasian ancestry dislike the adage, "The Spaniards conquered the New World, but the Indians conquered the Spaniards." This cultural reconquest, as it were, has molded the attitudes of the present population and is the basis of three problems that confront our hemispheric neighbors.

The first problem concerns the attitudes that should be assumed toward the native Indians and their cultures. The second deals with the attitudes of most of the countries toward the United States of America and other non-Latin American nations. The third revolves about the attitudes of the Latin American nations toward one another.

A North American myth concerning Latin American populations depicts them as being alike in such areas as language, economy, native culture, and the like. Such myths are frequently given support by superficial or irresponsible journalistic accounts, bad movies, travel posters, and inadequately informed tourists. Over the portals of Union Station in Washington, D.C., there is a Spanish adage to the effect that if you would gain the wealth of the Indies by going there, you must bring the wealth of the Indies with you. The Spaniards knew over 300 years ago that one had to possess understanding and empathy if one would profit by being in the New World.

The late Frank Tannenbaum, Columbia University professor and noted authority on Latin America, aptly wrote of Latin America that the whole is greater and more complex than the sum of its parts. He also confirmed that many of the individual nations themselves lack cultural unity within their own borders (63:147).

Latin American populations are deeply split between the cultured, urbane, and cosmopolitan minorities and the very large numbers of illiterate and semiliterate peasants and workers. The largest number of literate people are found in Chile, Costa Rica, Argentina and Uruguay. These four countries have the best public educational systems in Latin America. Coincidentally, Uruguay, Costa Rica and Argentina have an insignificant number of Indians and mestizos. Chile suppressed its Araucanians at the end of the last century and segregated them in the south. Until 1966, Chile had a more stable government and a smaller number of constitutional changes in its 150-year history than any of the others. In Mexico, Peru, and Brazil approximately 50 percent of the people are illiterate. In Central America, except for Costa Rica and Panama, illiteracy runs from 55 percent to 95 percent.

German Arcinegas pointed out in *Entre la Libertad y el Miedo* ("Between Liberty and Fear") (1952) that there are two Latin Americas: the visible one consisting of government and official organizations, and an invisible one consisting of the oppressed and downtrodden masses. Carlos Gutierrez, a Mexican reporter, wrote an article in 1967 for the *Sacramento Bee* (Calif.) entitled "Chasm Between Rich, Poor, Grows." It is significant that the conditions described in this article are from Mexico, a developing nation, not an underdeveloped one. Mexico used to be pointed to with pride by our Alliance for Progress and A.I.D. officials as *the* Latin American nation to be emulated by others.

The idea that Mexico is made of light and shadow, wealth and extreme poverty, culture and deep ignorance, is not new. But what is becoming more and more apparent is that the chasm between the small, privileged minority and the masses is going at a fast pace.

The not so casual observer will see that around those smoking chimneys, not far from the beautifully laid out developments, incongruous masses of humanity still are unaware that this is a developing nation, that the gross national product grew last year by six percent, that per capita income rose in 15 years from $230 to $450.

Still about sixty percent of its population is included in the peon class. . .officially there are more than 5,000 persons who earn more than one million pesos* a year—but, according to recently published statistics, the other group, the have nothings, is growing at a much faster pace. . .only 47 percent of the population uses shoes on a daily basis.

In Latin America there are whole Indian cultures that are still encapsulated and live within their separate and distinct worlds. What we call civilization and modernity are almost unknown to millions of Latin Americans and often not especially desirable to them. These cultures, traditionally authoritarian and hierarchical, still feel the heavy hand of the past. The street vendor of lottery tickets still addresses a

---

*1 peso (Mexican) = $.08 U. S. currency.

prospective customer in an automobile as *patrón*. A *patrón* in Latin America was, and is, more than a wealthy man. He was all-wise, a leader, a guide, and a protector of his people. He was the ruler of his domain, which might be a hacienda or his feudal village in any part of Latin America.

There are innumerable instances of the heterogeneity of the Latin American nations. A rather obvious one is the attitude of each nation toward its ethnic minorities. There is no uniform attitude. For instance, anti-Semitism exists in all countries among certain portions of the populace and bureaucracy to varying degrees although it is officially condemned by each government. It differs in the urban and rural areas and varies with each country. Argentina evidences the greatest amount of prejudice due, in part, to the presence of Arab propagandists. Argentina has one-half of the total number of Jews in Latin America. In rural areas it may be predicated on ignorance and a remnant of the preachings of priests who inveighed against Jews and pictured them as incarnate Satans. In many places off the beaten path, such as Ecuador, Guatemala, and the Yucatan Peninsula in Mexico, one finds the belief that Jews have horns and a tail. In many rural places on Good Friday, sparklers and other fireworks are used upon leaving church services and cries will be heard, *"Muerte a Judios,"* death to Jews. The original cry used the name of Judas, and at present the people do not know the difference between Judas and *Judios*.

Anti-Semitism is quite virulent in and about Buenos Aires and is growing in Guatemala. Cuba had the least amount of anti-Semitism. This writer made a sociological survey in 1969 of Cuban Jews residing in South Florida. (This survey is reported in the *American Jewish Year Book*, 1969 edition.) To a person, all those interviewed stated that anti-Semitism was nonexistent in Cuba although one might find one or two individuals who were antipathetic to Jews. The Cuban government's failure to permit the ship *St. Louis* and its almost 900 Jewish refugees who had fled Nazi Germany to land in 1939, was due to factors other than anti-

Semitism.* President Bru refused to recognize the visas held by the passengers because he had heard that the Cuban consuls in Europe had taken bribes varying from $500 to $1,000 for the issuance of each visa. Despite a positive attitude toward its Jewish citizens, Cuba voted more times against Israel in the U.N. on issues affecting that nation than any other country except the members of the Arab bloc. Cuba voted against Israel even when the Communist bloc was pro-Israel from 1947 to 1952. Of course, since 1960, Cuba has voted consistently with Russia and its satellites.

To understand the anachronism of the pre-1960 voting—lack of internal anti-Semitism but anti-Israel attitudes—one must know that most Latin American ambassadors to the U.N. are permitted to vote as they please unless they receive specific instructions from their Foreign Office on matters which are of concern to their nation. This makes accessibility, persuasion, and other forms of influence available to anyone interested in garnering votes.

Constitutions rarely provide a very reliable description of the realities of any Hispano-American government. In the context of this book, it is not profitable to study the various constitutions. Among the reasons militating against such discussion is the fact that many national constitutions are often ephemeral and short-lived. Ecuador had sixteen constitutions in the first 115 years of its sovereignty. The average life of most constitutions in Latin America has been less than twenty years.

Few people are aware of the deep antagonisms that exist among many Latin American nations. There are boundary disputes between Honduras and Guatemala; between land-locked Bolivia and Chile; between Venezuela and Surinam; and Peru resents the Chilenos for taking land from them in the War of the Pacific (1879–1883). This war between Bolivia and

---

Voyage of the Damned by Gordon Thomas and Max Morgan Witts (Stein & Day, 1974) is an excellent account of the ill-fated voyage.

Peru on one side and Chile on the other was a contest for possession of the Atacama Desert. Spain had never drawn a boundary between Chile and Peru. Prior to independence, Bolivia was a part of the viceroyalty of Peru. In 1830, it was learned that the desert had heavy deposits of sodium nitrate. Each of the three nations claimed part of the 600-mile-long desert. Chile, with British and German capital, was the first to exploit the entire area. It paid a royalty on the ore mined to Peru and Bolivia.

Peru began the trouble by seizing Chilean nitrate works and Bolivia joined in the fray by demanding higher royalties. Chile defeated both nations in the war. Peru was beggared and Bolivia lost its Pacific seacoast port and became land-locked. The Chaco War was begun in 1932 by Bolivia against Paraguay in order to secure an outlet to the Atlantic through the La Plata river system. Paraguay won the war "of the green hell." Argentina had supported Paraguay, and Chile the Bolivians.

There is a deep rivalry between Mexico and Argentina for commercial and political leadership in Latin America. The five-day war between Honduras and El Salvador in 1970 has left wounds that have not yet healed. Sports, boundaries, and the holding of jobs in Honduras by Salvadorians were among the causes of friction and resultant war.

While all Catholics are considered Roman Catholic, their Catholicity varies. This matter is discussed more fully in the chapter on religion. The charge is made against Mexico that it is atheistic because it has no Sunday "blue laws." There appears to be an unwritten rule since 1926 that no Mexican president ought to attend any religious services during his term of office. He may be seen in church to attend a baptism, a communion, or a wedding. Priests, monks and nuns are prohibited from wearing their clerical or religious garb on the public streets. The principal place where this law is adhered to is the capital, Mexico City.

The "War of the Cristeros" (1926-1929) was a battle between the Church and the Mexican government under the

then President Calles. Priests were found hanged from tele-
phone poles, churches were closed, sacraments were not given
publicly and religious pandemonium reigned. The American
Ambassador Dwight Morrow finally brought the parties
together. Monks, priests and nuns seen in their religious
regalia in Mexico City are usually visiting foreigners unaware
of the regulations, or are deliberately flaunting them.

Some nations have concordats with the Vatican and have
a modus vivendi on the manner of appointment of
bishops, the number permitted and birthplace qualifications
of the lower clergy. Some few nations still nominate their
own candidates for bishoprics and treat church property as
state-owned. Others, such as Brazil, "have begun to give
way—and, at an ever-accelerating rate—to one that is more
modern, more urban, more industrialized, more open, more
pluralistic, and more secular," according to Ilda S. Wiarda
and Howard J. Wiarda (69:13).

Protestants fare much better in many places than they do
in others. There is no uniformity. However, in Mexico and
Guatemala, in rural places and quite distant from the beaten
path, an average of twenty Protestants lose their lives each
year by the hands of fanatically driven local peasants.
Catholics attribute these assassinations to rural witches who
incite the people and they disown any role in this homicidal
activity of the local parish priest. In Mexico, Protestants
deliberately understate their membership so that the Catholics will not regard them as a menace. In many other places,
the Jew is preferred to the Protestant since Jews have no
missionaries and they do not proselytize due to Jewish
religious law which requires that a prospective convert is to
be dissuaded from fulfilling his intentions. The Jewish
communities, as do the Protestants, and for similar reasons,
underestimate the number of their adherents.

2 ● Geography and Language

Latin America ranges from the Rio Grande on the north to Tierra del Fuego on the south and from the Atlantic Ocean to the Pacific. (The Rio Grande, the boundary between the United States and Mexico, is known as the Rio Bravo in Mexico and some other Latin American countries.) For the past 150 years, Latin America was regarded as a culturally homogeneous area despite the fact that it is divided into twenty-three nations. The fiction of homogeneity is regarded as fact by many to this day. The United States' foreign policy subscribed to this view in 1961 when, under President John F. Kennedy, the Alliance for Progress was developed and almost thrust upon these nations. Briefly, the Alliance proposed that, in order to raise the standards of living of Latin Americans, and to provide cultural and educational advantages for the masses and other social benefits, the United States would obligate itself to contribute $2 billion a year for ten years. The Latin American governments agreed to improve their tax structures, make more than matching contributions to the programs that would be devised, and innovate other social and institutional changes.

There are some in "Foggy Bottom" who still hold to the view of one Latin America. The first high-level State Department admission that there were disparities among these nations came on March 6, 1968, when Covey T. Oliver, Assistant Secretary of State for Inter-American Affairs, reported to the U.S. Senate Foreign Relations Committee that "there are twenty-three nations involved, each with a unique political and social structure. . . ." He also admitted, somewhat belatedly, that "we must know the fundamental problems in each country, its political process and the forces that decide that process." However, he still betrayed a lack of knowledge of what has been written over the years when he stated, ". . . there is an inescapable socio-psychological dimension in international relations—one that I must say I wish received more attention from scholars and others whose words are heard or read abroad." Mr. Oliver apparently did not know that since 1962, scholars and others had been writing that the Alliance for Progress had died aborning and that A.I.D. (U.S. Agency for International Development) was an aberration of a bureaucratic mind and conceived in ignorance.

The term "Latin America" is regarded as a synonym for Mexico, Central and South America. (Mexico is part of North America.) Many Mexicans consider themselves *Americanos*, and differentiate themselves from us by calling us *Norteamericanos*. Simón Bolivar, the great Venezuelan liberator, referred to the peoples of South America in 1819 simply as *Americanos*. Michael D. Olien, historian-anthropologist of the University of Georgia, in his *Latin Americans: Contemporary Peoples and Their Cultural Traditions* writes that "some have placed such great emphasis on national differences that they deny there is a 'Latin America' " (45A:106). He divides the total area into four interaction spheres: Amerind-America which includes the lower half of Mexico, Guatemala, Ecuador, Peru and Bolivia; Afro-America which covers Cuba, Hispaniola, the three Guianas and the northeast section of Brazil as well as the eastern parts of Honduras, Salvador and Panama; Euro-America which includes Chile, Argentina, southern Brazil, Uruguay and Paraguay; Mestizo-America that covers northern Mexico, the major parts of Central American nations that are not Afro-America, Colombia, Venezuela, and the non-Afro-American part of Brazil and all of Argentina.

"Latin America, as a generality, may conjure up a mental image of people sharing Spanish as a common language—forgetting that Brazilians speak Portuguese, the Surinamese speak Dutch, that the people of former French Guiana speak French, as do those in several Caribbean islands, while others of the islanders, such as Jamaica and Barbados, speak English. [Many do not consider most Caribbean islands, except Cuba and Puerto Rico, as part of Latin America.] There are tens of millions in Central and South America who do not speak Spanish. In the permanent population of Latin America are also found Europeans, Orientals, Indians, and other Far Easterners. There are also the indigenous peoples, other than the Indians, whom Magnus Morner lists in his sixteen castes" (43:57). Some of them are as follows:

1. Spaniard and Indian beget mestizo.
2. Mestizo and Spanish woman beget castizo.
3. Spanish woman and Negro beget mulatto.
4. Spaniard and mulatto woman beget morisco.

(Moriscos is also the name for Moors in Spain who converted to Christianity after 1492 but secretly remained faithful to Islam.)

5. Mestizo and Indian woman beget cholo.
6. Negro and mulatto woman beget zambo.
7. Negro and Indian woman beget sambo de Indio.

Many of the foregoing and others do not consider themselves members of the various nation states. There is another question as to whether those who speak Spanish share a common meaning for words that they use.

The five nations of Central America, together with Mexico, were part of the viceroyalty of New Spain until they gained independence in 1821. The five provinces that are now the five Central American nations remained a part of Mexico until 1828 when they broke away and formed the United Confederation consisting of Guatemala, Salvador, Nicaragua, Honduras, and Costa Rica. This United Confederation came to an end in 1838. Since then the five have remained sovereign states. Attempts to form an economic union among them have met with little success. At the 1974 conferences to establish uniform prices on the bananas being exported from these countries (vulgarly known as Banana Republics) and Panama, only a short term agreement was arrived at, which then fell apart. In December 1970, Honduras broke away from the C.A.C.M., Central American Common Market. The C.A.C.M. was to be a conduit by which mutual aid would be utilized in exchanges of raw materials and exports of raw products, which include coffee as well as bananas. The Associated Press reported that on February 24th, 1975, the economic ministers of the five nations "were unable to reach agreement on cancelling unilateral trade measures directed against the common market partners." Restrictions had been placed on products imported from other C.A.C.M. members. The groups of products included shoes, clothing and textiles. Nicaragua imposed quotas on these imports from El Salvador and Guatemala "in violation of the rules of the C.A.C.M. which call for free trade among the member countries." Costa Rica had refused to eliminate its import quotas on the same above products from El Salvador and Guatemala.

Actually "Latin America" was a term created by the French in the middle of the nineteenth century to designate that part of the New World which did not have basically English roots. In this book, "Latin America" will be employed only as a geographical term, designating everything south of the Rio Grande, except the Caribbean islands and former foreign colonies—Dutch, British and French Guiana. The reasons for the exclusions are found in the history of these places, their cultures and languages. Cuba and Puerto Rico have many roots in Spanish culture but Puerto

Rico has closer connections with the United States and Cuba is, and has been, unique. Even prior to 1960 and Fidel Castro's rise to power, Cuba received scant attention in the history and other cultural courses in Latin American schools.

The indifference to Cuba prior to 1960 by most Latin American nations was due to the dominance of the United States in Cuban international affairs since under the Platt Amendment, which was part of the Cuban-United States Treaty of 1904, the United States was given almost total say in the island's foreign policy. In addition, American business interests held a dominant position in Cuba's economic life. The American base at Guatánamo was physical evidence of the American military presence on Cuban soil. The closeness to Florida contributed, prior to 1960, to what Floridians called "the Cuban invasion" because thousands came to Miami for vacations in July and August. Cuba did not share the animosity, envy, or jealousy of other Latin American states toward the United States.

Cuban Spanish is different from that spoken in other nations south of our border. A Panamanian once replied to my statement that I had difficulty in understanding Cubans when they spoke Spanish, *"No hablan espanol los Cubaños. Ellos lo comen."* ("The Cubans do not speak Spanish, they eat it.") This is due to the dropping of the "s" in the middle or at the end of words, their elisions, and their rapid, staccato speech. They are the only ones who call a bus, *guagua.* In other countries, *guagua* is an insect and in Colombia and Venezuela, it is an obscene word. *Papaya* is the Spanish and English word for a fruit. In Cuba, however, among the lower classes, it refers to a part of the female genitals. Cubans desiring papaya call for *fruta bomba.*

Hispanic America and Ibero-America will be used as synonyms for Latin America. Mexico, Central and South America (except for Brazil, Surinam and the Guianas) have collectively a population in excess of 225 million and a land area more than thrice the size of the United States. The land is blessed and cursed by mountain ranges. The Sierra Occidental is an extension of the Rocky Mountains and runs as far south as Panama. The Sierra Oriental begins in Mexico and ends in Guatemala. Between these two ranges lies the Valley of Mexico, which is 7,300 feet above sea level.

South America has the rugged Andean Range which runs down the entire west coast from Colombia to the tip of Chile and has a finger stretching eastward across Colombia and Venezuela. The Andes are truly the continental divider. These mountains reach three to four miles high and constitute an almost impossible barrier. They divide peoples from each other, permit cultures to flourish untouched by modern times, and exclude the millons who live atop or on the eastern flanks of the mountains from the dubious benefits of civilization.

Practically all rivers, except the Amazon, run east and west. The Amazon, 3,500 miles long, cuts a broad swath through Brazil, being fifty miles wide in some places. Its headwaters are in Colombia and northeastern Peru. The Amazon runs easterly through much of Brazil and then courses southward. The Orinoco rises in the Caribbean and runs in a southerly and easterly path.

The climate ranges from below freezing in the heights of the Andes and at the perpetually snowy tip of the South American continent to northern equatorial climates of unrelenting heat in the lowlands jungles and rainforests, especially from October to the following March of each year. (The seasons are the reverse of those north of the Equator.) In most of the area, the rainy season is the spring and summer. In Panama and the lowlands of Colombia and Brazil, there is an overabundance of water. There are desert regions in northern Mexico (an extension of the Mojave Desert) and in southern Peru, northern Chile and western Bolivia. The Gran Chaco, a desert, extends from Peru to Bolivia on the east and to Chile in the south. There are active and inactive volcanos. In Mexico there is Paricutin; in Costa Rica, Irazú and Arenal; and there is one in Corcovado, Chile. Earthquakes occur in too many places to mention. In brief, 25 percent of the total area is mountainous, 25 percent is swampy, and 10 percent is either desert or very dry.

The mountains, rivers, forests, and volcanos have created

many isolated areas throughout the central regions of South and Central America. This isolation is further perpetuated by lack of roads. Even where roads exist, means of transportation are inadequate. Furthermore, a lack of money bars the use of rudimentary public transportation systems where they do exist. Farming and life styles in most rural areas are on a subsistence level. The few cash crops—coffee, bananas, rice, and beans—are used to purchase necessities. Travelling is not one of them. This enforced isolation plays an important role in the political life of regions such as in Brazil inward from the Atlantic coast; on the eastern slopes of the entire length of the Andes; the southern parts of Colombia and Venezuela; and in the social, cultural, and economic lives of the inhabitants. Even language has been affected, causing words to have disparate nuances and meanings in different places.

A few words will illustrate this last statement. In Mexico, *ladino* means either a vernacular of Spanish used by Sephardi Jews in Spain just prior to 1492 and since then and in North Africa, Italy, Greece, and Turkey; or it may mean a person who can speak Spanish intelligibly; or a wily person. In Guatemala, it means a person of mixed racial decent (1:238). Richard N. Adams gives the foregoing definition, but he also defines the word as used during the colonial period: Indians who abandoned their native idiom and adopted Spanish customs.

To others, it means a white person born in the country. In Spain, according to the dictionary of the Royal Spanish Academy, it is defined, *"que habla con facilidad alguna o algunas lenguas además de la propia,"* "those who can speak one or more languages with ease, in addition to their native tongue." African slaves brought to the New World in the sixteenth century who learned to speak Spanish were called *negros ladinos.* They commanded a higher price. This is a good place to interpolate the derivation of the word "nigger." Our dictionaries state that the word is derived from the Spanish or French word *negro* meaning "black." That is incorrect. We must recall that the majority of the ships that brought the early Negro slaves from Africa were Dutch. The

Dutch word for black is *nikker,* and there is no pejorative connotation in the Dutch word.

In Mexico, Central America, and parts of South America, *mestizo* means "a person of mixed ancestry"—Indian and Spanish. In Peru and Bolivia, *cholo* has the same meaning, as does *Maturrango* in Argentina, while *chapetone* is a synonym for *cholo* in other places. *Apodar* means "to nickname" in all countries except Colombia and *apodo* is a "nickname." In Colombia *apodo* means "alias." All Latin Americans agree that the purest Spanish is spoken in Colombia or Peru. In Mexico City, when traffic lights turn red, the word *alto* is illuminated. It means "stop." In Chile and Argentina, *paré* is used. Other South Americans use *alto* in speaking to animals and regard its use for humans as an insult. *Madre* is the word for "mother," but the same word in Brazilian Portuguese means a "mixture of wine and vinegar," "a nun," "a mother superior," or an obscenity. In Cuba, they use *doblar* when they want to make a turn to the right or left in an auto, but in Mexico they use *voltear.*

Since some Habañeros use *madre* as a synonym for a loose woman, many of the lower economic classes, when inquiring about the health of a friend's mother, will not ask, *"¿Como está su mamá?",* but will inquire, *"¿Como está la Señora madre?"* The fish that Floridians call the red snapper is known as *huachinango* in Mexico and Central America, but *pargo* in Cuba and Puerto Rico. *Frijoles* means "beans" in Central and South America, but in Cuba beans are called *habas,* which happens to be the name for lima beans in Mexico. In Venezuela, *carrotas* means "beans" and in other countries *habichuela* is used; *judía* is a stringbean as well as the word for a Jewess.

There are three ways to use speech; intentionalism, extentionalism, and voice modulation—what the words mean to the speaker, what they mean to the auditor, and the mood or tone of the speaker. In Latin America, the pitch of the voice, the placing of the accent in each word on the proper syllable and the general manner are of prime importance. The extent of the Spanish vocabulary, except for the well-educated and cultured, is much more limited than that of the English vocabulary of an American who is the counterpart of the Spanish-speaking person. The use of the diminutive suffix *cita*—e.g., *mamacita* instead instead of *mama; pesita* instead of *peso*—illustrates the dual role of *cita* or *ita* as an addition of affection when appended to a word. *Pesita*, when used by a beggar or a retailer in negotiating a sale, implies that the value of the coin is so small that one should not hesitate to give it or haggle over it. Charles Kany, the philologist, wrote that ". . .the spoken standard speech of Spain differs in a number of respects from the spoken language of America—not that any uniformity exists in spoken American Spanish."

Many Americans believe that because of the hundreds, if not thousands, of cognates in English and Spanish, they have an extensive Spanish vocabulary. We invoke a caveat, "Don't trust cognates!" Two examples should suffice. There is a vast difference between "embarrass" (Eng.) and *embarazada* (Sp.). *Embarazada* means "pregnant." "Luxury" and *lujurioso* (the "j" having a guttural sound) are similarly distant in meaning. *Lujurioso* means "lustful," "lecherous," or "lewd," and it has no connection with "luxury."

Pedro Henríquez Ureña wrote, "There is no single Hispanic American language" (26:4). Gilbert Chase, professor at Tulane University, a linguist, added that there are five zones each employing different ways of speaking Spanish in the Americas: (1) Mexico and Central America; (2) the Caribbean area, which includes the Antilles, the greater part of Venezuela, and the Atlantic coast of Colombia; (3) the Andean region, which includes the southern part of Venezuela, and the greater part of Colombia, Peru, Ecuador, Bolivia, and northwestern Argentina; (4) Chile; and (5) the Rio de la Plata region, which covers most of Argentina, Uruguay and Paraguay. Of course, in Paraguay 50 percent of the people speak Guaraní, an Indian language. Even in Asunción, the capital, many Indian words have been added to Spanish.

Each zone and each nation within each zone has regional differences not only in pronunciation, but also in the meaning of words used. Some of these differences arose from the people who immigrated or were brought there from different areas. Although Spaniards predominated in every area during the colonial period (1521–1825), there were also other voluntary and involuntary immigrants. Negroes were brought in as slaves from Africa to Brazil, the coastal regions of Mexico and Central America, and Venezuela, as well as to the Caribbean Islands. The Negroes were able to work well in the oppressive heat and humidity and they supplanted the Indians on plantations. Spaniards and Portuguese intermarried with the Indians, or, in any case, sired their offspring.

The Tribunal of the Holy Office of the Inquisition in Portugal exiled the crypto-Jews (secret Jews, commonly termed *Marranos)* to Brazil where they were able to practice their faith almost openly. Jews controlled many of the provincial towns and villages in Brazil and northwestern Argentina. In the early 1630s, Jews controlled the trade and commerce of the Spanish viceroyalty of Peru. Peru then included all of Ecuador, Peru, Bolivia, Chile, part of Colombia and most of Argentina. On the other hand, the Spanish throne and inquisitors in Spain barred from the Spanish New World possessions the Jews and their descendants to the fourth generation even if they had converted. All their decrees, the last issued as late as 1803, were ineffective in preventing Jews from establishing themselves in the Spanish and Portuguese colonial empire. These Jews came from various European states, and Protestants from Europe also migrated to the New World.

The Spaniards brought Negroes from Africa—as did the Dutch and Portuguese—and Orientals from the Philippines, China and Japan to their colonial empire. The Portuguese brought slaves from Africa and India. Stanley Rycroft reported that "the different amalgamations, or combinations, of the Spanish, Indian, and Negro have produced the national psychology of each country, with all the variations due to the preponderance of one group or another. Subsequent immigrations from many parts of the world have further accented this racial composite. . .[accentuated by] climate and physical environment" (31A:49). In the nineteenth century many Orientals came voluntarily from the Far East, sometimes as hired hands for British companies that were building railroads in Mexico and Central America. All of these people have influenced the character of the people and their language and its inflection. An example is the word *mariachi*, which now refers to members of a group of strolling musicians. The word is derived from the French word *mariage*, an event at which such musicians performed as part of an entertainment.

Another important factor contributing to the character and variety of Latin-American Spanish was the languages of the indigenous people, the Indians, who were conquered. (Of course, even the English language has been enriched by such Indian words as "chocolate," "tomato," etc.) Since the Indian languages varied, the words adopted or absorbed into Spanish varied. In the Summer Institute of Linguistics in Chiapas, Mexico, twenty-seven different tongues, Mexican and Guatemalan, are studied. Peru, Brazil, Colombia, Bolivia, and Ecuador have large Indian populations, and they also speak many different tongues.

Only in nations such as Argentina or Costa Rica is there an absence of words of Indian origin, because 90 to 95 percent of the peoples are descended from European Caucasians. Chile should be added to these two because there the Indians met a fate similar to that which befell the American Indians during the period when it was believed that "the only good Indian is a dead Indian." Chileans, however, have not forgotten the Araucanians, indigenous Chilean Indians, who fought so valiantly until the nineteenth century for release from Spanish bondage. Their descendants are few, and they live in the southern part of Chile.

In addition to Spanish, the following are a few of the languages spoken—Portuguese (colorfully enriched by African words brought by Negro slaves) in Brazil, Quechua, Maya, Aymara in Ecuador, Peru and parts of Bolivia, and Guaraní. Once out of Asunción, Paraguay, more that 60 percent of the so-called Spanish is composed of words from

Guaraní. Guarani is the second official language. In addition to these there are over 150 Indian tongues unrelated to each other, which, in the aggregate, are spoken by ten or fifteen million who know only their own Indian idiom. There are towns on main highways in Chiapas, Yucatán, Chihuahua, Durango, Lower California, Guatemala, Peru, Ecuador, Bolivia, and in the interiors of Brazil and Chile where many know little or no Spanish or Portuguese.

Since Latin contributed so heavily to both English and Spanish, it is to be expected that many words in both languages originate from the same source or root. This both helps and hinders recognition and understanding. There are many cognates in Spanish and English that cause confusion for Latins who migrate to the United States. For instance, for the words "notary public" used in America, Cuba uses *notario,* while the rest of Spanish America has a *notario público.* In the United States, a notary public is an administrative person authorized to perform certain routine acts such as administering an oath to a person executing an affidavit or acknowledging the signatures on real estate documents. In all Latin American countries, he is an important government official and has greater prestige and standing than a lawyer. The Florida Bar had to commence several proceedings for the unlawful practice of law against former Cuban notaries who had migrated or been brought to the United States on the Freedom Flights and had qualified to become notary publics (available to almost any applicant in Florida) and thought, as did their clients, that they had the same privileges in Florida that they had had in Cuba, which included the practice of law.

Although the words "democracy" and "republic" are similar in both languages, they have different nuances in English and Spanish. The word "excuse" sounds very similar to the Spanish *excusado.* In Spanish, the latter means "unnecessary," or a "toilet," or "water closet." The words "respect" in English and *respeto* in Spanish are cognates. The words are simply defined in Spanish and English dictionaries as exact translations of each other. Here the dictionaries are of no help since there are variances in the connotations to people north and south of the border.

Several years ago, two psychiatrists, Dr. Rogelio Díaz Guerrero of Mexico and Dr. John Peck of Texas, framed twenty questions to determine what a group of cognate words meant to Mexican and American university students. The interviewees were from the Mexican National University and the University of Texas. Approximately 300 students from each school were selected in groups that were matched chronologically and in courses of study. The two doctors were bilingual, and the test papers were checked by each for possible deviations in each language since the test was in the native language of each group.

Of all the words tested, the most glaring differences in interpretation of meaning occurred in the words "respect" and *respeto*. In only one of the twenty questions asked concerning the words "respect" or *respeto* were the answers of the two groups identical. There were divergences in nineteen. The Mexican students do not respect their equals or their peers or their social and economic inferiors. They extended respect primarily to those who could exert power and authority, or to those to whom they were under obligation. There was an undertone of obsequiousness in the Mexican's respect. The Americans respected their equals. Power, authority, and obligation were not factors in the respect of Americans.

An elementary lesson in learning Spanish is that there are two forms of the English word "you." The two singular forms are *tú* and *usted*. The first is used for children and other family members, lovers, one's friends, and employees, while the second is used in speaking to strangers or for formal purposes. There is a built-in class consciousness in these two words that plays an important role in the social and economic segregation that exists throughout Hispano-America. A child uses *tú* toward all household servants and his peers but *usted* for his parents, teachers, and all adult relatives. Many adolescents over sixteen begin to use *tú* toward all those who are of a social or economic status inferior to that of their families.

While class consciousness will be discussed in other contexts, it is appropriate to mention here that an understanding of role differentiation according to class is a *sine qua non* in Latin America. It is imperative to gaining any and all insights to the Latin American mind.

For many years nursing ranked so near the bottom of the scale that only uneducated girls became nurses (13:48). This attitude has changed only slightly. The tasks of handling bedpans and washing bodies are considered menial and dirty. The low status of nurses may be a remnant of the fact that during the colonial period the Inquisitors sentenced females to serve as orderlies in the hospitals.

A señora takes her maid with her when she goes to the supermarket so that the maid can carry the packages. *Gente decente,* decent people, refuse to carry packages in public (33:300) except in Argentina or southern Brazil. While Americans who hold managerial posts have no hesitancy in pitching in and using their hands and brawn in times of need, their Latin counterparts would consider this stepping out of role, a loss of status.

Since the word "integration" will be used many times, and is a cognate for the Spanish *integración,* it should be understood that despite the dictionaries, the two words do not have identical meanings; the Latin American word is richer in concepts. Integration, or *integración* in Latin America, includes a person's changed perspective of the world, better relations between the sexes, bringing the marginal peasant and slum dweller into the economic national stream as job-holders, ecumenicalism between the leaders of different faiths, the creation of a common market for nations, the development of effective labor unions, and innumerable other human and international relationships (60:vii, viii).

We will not go into concepts of time, which are completely different from ours and, if not understood, can rupture relationships between Americans and Latins. For instance, a formal invitation in Chile to a wedding or fiesta may read, *"a las ocho horas,"* ("at 8 o'clock"), without any qualifying words. This means that you are expected any time after 10:00 P.M. If, however, the invitation or announcement reads, *"a las ocho horas ingles,"* that means that you are expected to arrive promptly at 8 o'clock because English time is indicated.

"Segregation" is a cognate for *segregación,* and here again there are differences in the nuances of the word in the two languages and also the ratiocination of the Spanish word. Latin Americans delight in stating that color segregation does not exist in their lands and that they are free of the segregation problems that plague the United States. The first part of the statement is true, but only to a degree. Color may not be the cause of segregation as is practiced in many parts of our country, but segregation exists even in Brazil, the most highly integrated of all Latin American states. No president of Brazil has been a Negro, nor has a governor of any of the five most important states of that country ever been a black or Negro. There is no Negro in the highest echelons of the military. In the United States, we spell "Negro" with a capital "N," but in Latin America a small "n" is used.

The Brazilian sociologist, Gilberto Freyre, offers an interesting explanation for the absence of color prejudice in his country. Even a cursory analysis of the writings of this great libertarian reveals the debatable tolerant nature of the following statements. He wrote, "as the Brazilian attitude is one of large tolerance toward people who have African blood [whatever that may mean since there is no difference between the blood of whites and blacks] but who can pass for white, nothing is more expressive than the popular saying, 'anyone who escapes being an evident negro [sic] is white'" (15:19). Freyre admits that segregation of "social distance" exists because of class consciousness. He attributed miscegenation to the lack of Brazilian concern about color. Some of the most beautiful women in Brazil are those with a *café au lait* complexion. In fact, they are some of the most beautiful women in the world. They are not considered black in Brazil.

In the article, "The Human Race in Brazil," Robert A. Christopher reported that the 1948 number one hit song of the famous Rio de Janeiro Carnival preceding Lent was *"A Mulata e a Tal,"* "The Mulatto Is Tops" (32:168).

Many blacks are residents of the *favelas* or slums in Rio de Janeiro. The *favelas* are worse than the most squalid ghettoes in the United States. They perch precariously on the hills surrounding the city. Squatters live in these *favelas* which are noted for a lack of elementary sanitation. They live on gleanings from garbage, from petty theft, and in defiance of all authorities. (Similar squatter settlements with equally degrading conditions for humans are called *barriadas* in Lima, Peru, and *ranchos* in Caracas, Venezuela.

Freyre is correct in stating that "miscegenation has not led to degeneration in Brazil" since men stemming from ethnic and dual-colored amalgamations have been, and are, among the political and cultural leaders. In other Latin American countries, the antipathy, or prejudice, toward people of color—black, red or brown—was markedly present among the leading literary figures of the last century and for the first three decades of this one. The sad and unfortunate forebear of racism of Latin America was the great liberator himself, Simón Bolívar; "for him the 'people of color' were ungovernable." Their history, said he, would cause them to take "license for liberty, treachery for patriotism, and vengeance for justice" (16A:79,80). Stanford University's Professor John J. Johnson, noted Latin American historian, in his biography of Bolívar, commented that "the case for a common culture was no more sustainable during the Independence Era than it is today" (p. 69).

The Argentinian, Carlos Octavio Bunge, gave evidence of the arrogance and racism of the Spaniards when he wrote in 1918 of the lack of meaningful attainment by Negroes, and classified their typical traits as "servility and vanity" (35:17). Bunge wrote in the most disparaging terms not only of Negroes, but also of mulattoes and mestizos, who were known in some parts of South America as *chapetones*. He attributes the success of *caciquismo,* political bossism, to the servility and fatalism of all nonwhites (35:18). *Cacique* is the Indian word for "chief." It is now used throughout Latin America. The *cacique* is the all-powerful leader of the tribe and serves as judge and final arbiter. *Caciquismo* is the absolute rule of local political bosses.

The Bolivian, Alcides Arguedas, wrote *Pueblo Enfermo*, "The Sick People," which accuses his countrymen of bringing national backwardness and political chaos to the nation because of inheritance and environmental forces. The "inheritance" stems from the Indian ancestry and the "inclination" of the mestizo or cholo to sloth and inebrity and to his atavistic traits (61:20). Almost the entire chapter, "The Sick Continent," in Stabb's *In Quest of Identity* deals with South American and Mexican authors who attributed the "illness" of Latin America to the preponderance of "inferior" non-European races in their midst (61:21).

The psyche of the Spaniard has been excellently described by C. Harvey Gardner in his *Martin Lopez: Conquistador Citizen of Mexico* (Lexington, Ky., 1958). He states, "Intellectually he was ever a man at war with himself—simultaneously the realist and the idealist, the conserver and the changer, the age-old Spaniard and the emergent American. Imaginative and conforming, consistent and inconsistent, generous and greedy, cultured and crude, aggressive and passive, rapacious and considerate, exaggerating and truthful, indolent and ambitious, cooperative and contentious, simple and complex—of such was the contradictory nature of Martin Lopez" (17:6).

The Indians of Mesoamerica also possessed what we would classify as dichotomies in their psyche. On the one hand we find that Aztecs could tear the pulsating hearts from live human sacrifices, while an Aztec mother could advise her daughter "to live with much prudence and circumspection . . . and see that you live in the world in peace, tranquility and contentment . . . and may you come to God, who is in every place" (cf. Prescott's *Conquest of Mexico*, Appendix II, p. 715). The amalgam of the psyches of the Spaniard and

Indian has created or produced truly a "new race" which is incomprehensible to themselves as well as to all non-Latin Americans. José I. Rasco, in commenting on Luis Alberto Sanchez's book, *Existe América Latina,* stated, ". . . what is the essence of Latin America? . . . we have not yet given enough thought to what we really are." He quoted Leopold Zea, "A characteristic of man in the New World has been to emulate others in order to find himself."

3 ● The Latin American Search for Identity

The great Latin American literary figure and diplomat, Octavio Paz, asked in 1959, "What are we, and how can we fulfill our obligations to ourselves as we are?" He then added, "The history of Mexico is the history of a man seeking his parentage, his origins" (47:9).

For many years, Mexicans have been involved in a search for identity. This search has been termed *México y lo Mexicano*, "Mexico and the Mexicano." Inherent in the title is the question, "Who is the Mexican?" In Argentina, another study has been under way. They are considering the question, "Why is Argentina beset by unstable governments, military rule, palace revolts, etc.?" The questions disturb and puzzle the intellectuals of Argentina since their people are more European than those in other Latin American countries and appear to be more homogeneous than elsewhere, and they lack Indian or mestizo roots. The percentage of white ancestry* in

---

*More than 55 percent of the population are of Italian and Spanish descent and are no more than third or fourth generation Argentinians. They and Uruguayans constitute the most homogeneous white population in South America.

the Argentinian population is second only to Costa Rica among Latin American countries.

The same questions might be posed in practically all other Latin American countries. Brazil may be added to Argentina, Uruguay, and Costa Rica as exceptions to the typical variegated population groups because Brazil is Portuguese and Indian in origin and its history is radically different from that of the other countries. Among other differences are that Brazil has more registered Catholics in its population and is the only Latin American nation that has no divorce laws. While Brazil may have the most heterogeneous population, integration is more nearly a fact there than elsewhere. The Portuguese had no phobias about miscegenation.

The problem of identity, arising from a mixture of different ethnic groups, causes Latins to overindulge in self-analysis. The desire for self-knowledge exists primarily among the affluent and the intellectuals. However, self-understanding might reveal the need for change, and to traditionalists, change implies a loss of anchors and valued traditions. The fear of venturing into the unknown fills many with trepidation. The traditionalists of all groups fear loss of identity. North Americans believe that the world can be, and must be, changed; but Latin Americans believe that the world (including themselves) can be redeemed. To make a sacrifice for a betterment of life or the future is almost incomprehensible. We exclude the desire of the wealthy to become richer and the desire of the political leaders to have their countries become more powerful and more nationalistic. Latin Americans believe or suffer from the delusion that they are people of spirituality while Americans are materialistic.

Mexico has the largest Spanish speaking population. In many respects its problems are representative of those besetting the other nations. F. S. C. Northrup felt that it illustrates the Latin American component of Pan-American problems (45:10). This is one of the reasons why Mexico may be used, disproportionately, to corroborate some generalities.

Carlos Fuentes, a noted Mexican writer, around 1966, reviewed a book, *Hopscotch*, by the Argentinian novelist

Julio Cortazar. Fuentes reported that Cortazar left his land because "he was no longer capable of working within the stifling chauvinism, the provincial options, and the literary cannibalism of the real down-under, the metaphysical underground that is Spanish America." Fuentes stated that Latin America has a schizophrenic culture because it is torn between nostalgia for the noble savage and the eschatological yearning for the man who revolted. He uses pairs of words or phrases to describe Latins: "provincial attachment and cosmopolitan rootlessness; tequila against champagne; extreme individualism and apocalyptic collectivism; pride in anarchy and profound subservience before power; the gaucho makes his own laws, but El Señor Presidente can solve all problems." In other words, we are constantly confronted with conflicting absolutes in studying Latin American culture and people.

In the United States we call October 12, Columbus Day, for Christopher Columbus, the man whose deed we commemorate and who never touched our shores. In Latin American countries, the man is known by his correct name, Cristobal Colón, and October 12 is celebrated as *El Dia de la Raza*, "the Day of the Race." This celebrates the day on which a new race was born as a result of the Spaniards coming to the New World and having sexual relations with the aboriginal women. For more than 200 years, mostly without benefit of marriage, succeeding generations were the progenitors of a new race—a *mezclada*, a mixture of Spaniard and Indian, called the mestizo. The mestizo is a hybrid because it is not known with whom his ancestors mated. There is a whole series of names for the offspring of parents who are mestizos (in Spanish the male plural is the generic term for both sexes); mestizo and Negro; Spaniard and Negro; Negro and Oriental, and so forth. In current usage, however, all people of mixed racial ancestry fall under the generic category of mestizo.

The mestizo of Mexico and the cholo of Bolivia and Peru may regard themselves as Mexican, Bolivian, or Peruvian, and are more cognizant of their nationality than of racial origins, but their consciousness of the meaning of *political* nationality is minimal. Many mestizos of the lower economic classes deny knowledge of the word mestizo. Mestizos comprise the majority of the population in Mexico and Central America (except for Costa Rica), and most of South America (except for Netherlands Antilles, Chile, and Argentina). In Guatemala, Peru, Ecuador, and Bolivia, the Indian is in the majority "regardless of what official statistics say" (63:40).

Trying to use Latin American statistics approaches an exploration of some kind of never-never land. Luis Alberto Sánchez says that Peruvian statistics are poetry. Ex-Senator Gruening, who was a journalist and author before he entered politics in the late 1930s, wrote an excellent book, *Mexico and Its Heritage* (23). In it he says that one can believe anything said about Mexico regardless of how contradictory the statements may be. Each statement is true of something, somewhere.

Another authority said that there are three classes of statistics in Latin America: governmental, private industry, and impartial. Jaime Plenn in his book, *Mexico Marches,* concluded that the first two can be discarded immediately, and, as for the third, one should wait two years to test its probity. Professor John J. Johnson of Stanford University served as Acting Chief of the South American Branch of the Division of Research for the United States State Department (1952–53). He wrote that "the unreliability of statistics from most public and private agencies in Latin America is well known. I recommend allowance of 10 to 15 percent for error" (29:ix). University of California Professor James W. Wilkie, in his article, "Statistical Indicators of the Impact of National Revolution on the Catholic Church in Mexico, 1910–1967," shows that the Mexican government population figure for 1967 is 45,671,000, while the demographers of the Church give the figure of 39,816,020, almost six million less than the official number (71:99).

William L. Schurz noted that "official estimates are of doubtful credibility" (59:51). Thomas V. Greer of Louisiana State University, wrote, "The majority of intellectuals believe the literacy figures are adjusted after they arrive in

Mexico City." As one noted historian said to the author, "Mexican statistics are political statistics" (26:466).

From the very beginning of Spanish dominion over the New World, the *gachupin* and the *criollo* or *ladino* looked down upon the mestizo. The gachupin was a pure Spaniard born in Spain, while the criollo was a child born in the New World of gachupin parents. The distinction arising from place of nativity is a key element in the framing of the attitudes toward Spain of large segments of the Hispanic American peoples. The word "criollo" should not be confused with "creole" as used in the United States. Our creoles are the descendants of French or Spanish of mixed parentage and are usually from Louisiana and surrounding areas. The term is also applied to those of mixed parentage in the West Indies.

The mestizos are the most important segment of the Latin American population, not only because they constitute the largest percentage of the total populace, but also because they are the Latin Americans of tomorrow. The spread of mass communication must ultimately lead to their enlightenment and a consciousness of a collective political strength. Although less than the majority of the mestizos live in the cities, it is the urban mestizo who is being rapidly brought into the twentieth century through education and radio and TV. The near future will limn him as the man who will guide the destinies of the various nations. He is the man with whom the world will have to deal. He will not emerge in each country as an exact replica of the others, but, generally, his similarities will be great.

The mestizo is the dominant influence in Latin America (63:43). For 300 years (1521-1821) he constituted a despised class and was regarded as an inferior person, unstable, lazy, shiftless, and untrustworthy. Octavio Paz characterizes modern Mexicanism or mestizoism as carelessness, pomp, negligence, passion and reserve. He added that mestizos delight in the use of artistic forms (24:13).

The mestizo is willing to think about and to gaze upon

horror and death with equanimity. This is part of his philosophy: *no vale nada la vida*, life has no value. (The Spanish double negative does not make the affirmative as in English.) The mestizo combines his cult of life style and cult of death without difficulty, because death is part of life. Although religion is discussed elsewhere in this book, we note here that many Latins subconsciously see the bleeding and humiliated Christ as a transfiguration of themselves. Jesus was tried and condemned by an unfriendly court, and in His last moments, the soldiers caused His blood to flow. While under 300 years of Spanish rule, Indians and mestizos were degraded, were unjustly punished, and were treated with disdain, and their women defiled. They readily identify themselves with the suffering of Jesus.

The mestizo has been called *pelado*, literally "plucked" or "bare" or "nobody," and, according to Samuel Ramos, pelado is the designation of a universally familiar social type (31:57). Fernando Benítez wrote of the mestizo or pelado that he was "begotten with violence and without joy." He comes painfully into the world and is the result of the violence and cupidity of the Spaniard (40:325). For hundreds of years the mestizo lived marginally. He looked down upon the Indian and was ashamed of his Indian ancestry because he saw that the Indian was a slave, was treated contemptuously, was used and abused by the Church.

The Indian bedmate had little lasting sexual satisfaction from the lusty Spaniard who despised the creature upon whom he vented his lust. The *muchacha* or *criada*, the servant girl of today who is a mestiza, experiences little or no pleasure from her sexual experience when married. The husband indulges in no foreplay to intercourse with his spouse. The wife dare not evidence any sexual pleasure.

The personality of a lower-class mestizo may be characterized in this fashion: (a) he has two personalities, a real one and a fictitious one; (b) the real personality is inhibited; (c) the fictitious personality is the outer one, the one for the public to see. Its role is to transform any state of depression felt by the inner man from the real into a gayer and fantasy-like psychological state so that life becomes more bearable; (d) since the fictitious personality has no real basis, the situation creates a lack of self-confidence in the individual; (e) this insecurity then produces attitudes that appear to be abnormal symptoms, such as a baseless distrust of other people; though it seems to defy logical explanation, he is projecting onto others the role that he would assume were he in the other's place; (f) since he knows that he is living in a false world in which he cannot allow his real self to appear, he impairs his entire psychological structure and lives with severe inner tensions which frequently find violent outlets.

Sadism is almost endemic in the Latin American mestizo. Bullfighting, for all its artistry, grace and the poignant, dramatic moment of truth, is a form of sadism. The spectators mentally interpret and symbolize the entry of the sword into the bull as a form of satisfaction of their unfulfilled desires, ambitions, aspirations and aversions, and, some add, sexual gratification.

Many Americans are surprised to learn from Latin American doctors that the incidence of ulcers is as high, if not higher, as in the United States, and that heart conditions are rampant. Mexico has a homicide rate second only to Italy. There are several reasons for this, but of prime importance is that the dominance of the false role is a repressant on passions, which, in the absence of any catharsis or sublimation, causes an ultimate eruption in violence. Most Latins usually appear to be quiet, calm, phlegmatic, and polite. This is the outer personality.

The urban mestizo is making small beginnings in freeing himself from his inferiority complex. He feels the influence of his children who are receiving some education; inadequate as it may be it is more than he received; his contacts with the larger world and the impact of radio and TV are bringing an awareness to him that he is a person with rights. In the capital cities, he meets tourists from foreign countries who treat him with respect. Some of his friends trade with the tourists and he hears their stories of how foreigners can be "fleeced," which elevates his ego.

The efforts of the governments and some private groups to bring about a revival of pre-Colombian culture is of great interest to tourists and many foreign anthropologists and archeologists. Mexico and Peru have been the leaders in this endeavor to lay greater stress on Indian ancestry than on Spanish. One of the motivations for such efforts was to arouse pride of the mestizo in his ancestry, his country, and ultimately, in his nation. The revival has stimulated tourist interest in various areas of Guatemala and Panama as well as in Mexico and Peru. These places include such former Indian habitations as Palenque and the Yucatan Peninsula in Mexico, the islands inhabited by the San Blas Indians in Panama, Chichicastenango and Tikal in Guatemala, Machu Pichu and Cuzco in Peru. The museums in all of the countries attract many visitors.

Whether there is a success in having the mestizo relate himself to his Indian ancestry is questionable. When the antics of a driver of an automobile arouse the ire of the driver of another car, one of the insults that may be hurled at the offender is to call him *"Indio!"*—Indian.

Prior to the present generation, the indigenous peoples were usually short, olive skinned, and thin. This was due to the limited diet and its lack of vitamin content. Those Indians who ate tortillas (not used in South America) usually had good teeth because in the process of making the *massa*, the dough, the corn kernels are soaked in lime water. The legs of the men were short and very muscular. The women were as tall as the men and their bodies tended toward what we would term plump. Except for their walk, they exhibited little grace in their movements.

In modern times, the diet of beans, tortillas, rice, and small quantities of fowl or meat has been enlarged to include eggs, some dairy products, fruits, and vegetables. This has produced taller people. Indians have little or no body hair and one is hard put to see a stout Indian. The mestizo whose genes and chromosomes are predominantly those of his Indian forebears consequently has little or no body hair. It is not an uncommon sight to see men with straggly mustaches, the hairs of which are capable of being counted. Mestizas, of the lower classes especially, refrain from using a depilatory or shaving the hair on their legs so that this hair, like that of the men, evidences Caucasian ancestry. The father of one of our maids was a handsome mestizo with the typical picayune hirsute adornment on his upper lip. One day she was asked how often her father shaved. She replied that he shaved once in two weeks, but that he was really showing off since he could go a month before the hairs on his cheeks became really noticeable.

The mestizo avoids responsibility; this avoidance is not due to any inability to perform tasks. It arises from the fear that something may go wrong and he will be held responsible. A maid will never say, "I dropped the cup and it broke." She will use the reflexive and say, *"Se cayó y se rumpió la taza,"* "The cup fell by itself and broke itself."

The psyche of the mestizo is the result of the attempt to conceal an inferiority complex, according to Samuel Ramos (55:58). Ramos contends that the pelado "belongs to the most vile category of social fauna; he is a form of rubbish from the great city. He is less than a proletarian in the economic hierarchy, and a primitive man in the intellectual one." Paz gives three reasons for the mestizo trait of seeming to be unable to tell the truth: the mestizo delights in fantasy, he is desperate, or he wants to rise above the sordid facts of his life (47:23). The mestizo will lie and continue to lie even when he is aware that you know that he is lying.

The mestizo has lived in an open society since the end of World War I. While generally not accepted in the upper ten or 15 percent of the social structure, if he achieves affluence or political office this aids in piercing the social barriers. The mestizos exert power in several countries due to their high military posts. The armed forces were always open to the lower social levels and afforded an ease of mobility. The navy in Chile is a glaring exception to the foregoing statement. The Chilean navy was a special reserve for the scions of the oligarchy. In Peru, the Central American nations and Mexico one is hard put to find a "pure white" face among the ranks of the senior officers. The military juntas that run Bolivia, Peru, Brazil and Chile are composed of a majority of mestizos.

The mestizo accepts the Indian into his society provided that the Indian speaks Spanish, discards his native dress, wears European or American style clothes, eats the same foods as the mestizo, and conducts himself according to the social mores of the mestizos.

Despite all of the wars in the Pan American nations, the people are, to a large extent, the slaves of their past. James L. Busey, professor of political science at the University of Colorado, affirms that in Latin America the pattern of politics is interwoven with historical, physical, cultural, and the social environments in which they occur.

In Mexico there was the "Era and the Wars of Reform." This era ran from 1857 to 1867 and includes the war to remove Maximilian as emperor of Mexico and to abolish the empire that France imposed upon Mexico. Napoleon had sent his army in 1862 ostensibly to collect Mexico's debt to France. The French occupied the customs houses and seized all customs. Then Napoleon sent Maximilian to occupy the new throne created by the French. The United States was preoccupied with its own Civil War between the years 1862-1865. It was for this reason that Abraham Lincoln did not then invoke the Monroe Doctrine. However, he did do so in 1865. The Mexican army defeated Maximilian and his two top generals and executed them in Querétaro on the Hill of the Bells on June 19, 1867. Maximilian's fall was due to the French abandonment of him, especially after Lincoln's note of displeasure at Maximilian's presence, and the Mexican clergy's antagonism toward him because he was a liberal.

The Mexican Revolution (1910-1915) is analogous to our Civil War. The Revolution was initiated by Francisco I.

Madero and others to terminate the dictatorship of Porfirio Díaz (1876-1910). Díaz had bankrupted the country, permitted foreign investors to rape the country economically, and suppressed all attempts of the workers to organize and seek better working conditions. During the actual fighting of the Revolution, 1912-1915, Mexican fought against Mexican and it is estimated that one million Mexicans were killed. Following the victory in which Pancho Villa, Venustiano Caranza, and Emiliano Zapata became folk heroes (Caranza fell into disfavor later because while he was President, he was caught attempting to flee with the national treasury), a constitutional assembly representing the intellectuals and masses labored for two years and finally produced the Constitution of 1917. Since 1920, every Mexican president has served his full term and there has been an orderly succession of executives.

The Mexican Revolution liberated the mestizo and gave him a new status. His folk heroes were the mestizos, Villa and Zapata, who had overthrown Díaz and his cohorts. The mestizo now had the right to vote and the vicious *hacendado* system was broken. The practice of compelling the peons who slaved on the hacienda lands to make their purchases from the hacienda store, pay exorbitant interest, and inflated prices began to be a thing of the past. However, despite the distribution of land by successive presidents, the financial lot of the *campesinos*, rural farmers and workers, has not been greatly improved, although the government has distributed seed and made government loans to purchase tractors and other farm equipment. The *ejido* system, a form of communal settlement and farming, comparable in many respects to the Israeli kibbutz, has not met with the success that its progenitors had expected. Only about 25 percent of Mexican land is arable and much remains to be done in order to irrigate it.

Prior to 1910, it was said that "Mexico was the mother of the foreigner and the stepmother of the Mexican." During the era of Porfirio Díaz, known as Porifirismo, the British and Americans were permitted to make vast investments and had almost sovereign rights over their properties. During the present period Mexicans are taking over more and more foreign businesses and foreign firms are compelled to use Mexican made products, e.g. automobiles must have at least 65 percent "Made-in-Mexico" parts. This contributes to the new status of mestizos who not only are no longer outcasts but are an important segment of their country's economic and national pride.

The character of the Spaniard had great impact on the New World. In addition to imposing his language and culture on the inhabitants of the New World, he bequeathed and imparted some of his traits. The Spanish conquistador was infinitely courageous and infinitely greedy and often sadistic. The outstanding characteristic of the Spaniard is the dichotomy of his existence. He is ambivalent. Salvador de Madariaga, in his book, *Englishman, Frenchman and Spaniard* (38:42-2), shows that his countrymen defy single word definitions. He uses antonyms to describe the Iberian: hard and human, resigned and rebellious, energetic and indolent. The New World people were inculcated with some of these traits, and their awareness of this produced resentment. Leopold Zea in *The Latin American Mind* wrote of the problems of the nineteenth and twentieth centuries:

> The Hispanic American, upon analyzing himself, found that he was a man of many contradictions, and because he felt incompetent of effecting a synthesis of these contradictions, he chose the easiest way out, amputation. . . . He regarded the past as the root of all his misfortunes. . . . He surrendered to the difficult task of no longer being that which he was, in order to become, as if he never existed, something entirely different. . . . We carry our defects in our blood. . . . The past was, and still is, the colony.[46:8]

Fernando Benítez, in his *Los Primeros Mexicanos*, "The First Mexicans," wrote,

> The weakness of the Mexican and his serious limitations are attributable to the fact that he was born in a colony. He breathes an air of a land that was owned by a landlord, owing to certain divine and political imperatives. . . . The colony is closer to us

than we think. The deep sense of worthlessness, the Mexican's
famous inferiority complex . . . is an offshoot of the colony. . . . The colonial world has vanished, but not its fears,
distrust, suspicion. [3:278–281]

Prior to 1911, 20 percent of the population of most Latin
American nations, almost all white, were rich, and 80 percent,
mestizo and Indian, were poor. Presently, the proportion is
almost identical except that there is now a middle sector
comprising about 5 percent of the total populace, and 75
percent are now poor. (In 1967, Alberto Garcia Duarte, head of
the Mexican National Securities Commission, informed a
meeting of the Second Congress of American Stock Exchanges
that 10 percent of the people in Mexico receive about 90
percent of the national income.) The 20 percent who are in the
upper economic strata include many nonwhites who arrived
at this status via politics and important official roles, or who
are descendants of the pre-Revolutionary rich who remained
within the charmed circle, or those who intermarried with the
new heroes and powerful politicos. The change of faces in the
influential and decision-making group brought hope to those
who lived in feudal squalor in the first decade of this century.
As Latin America has industrialized and the great movement
from rural to urban areas has accelerated (mainly in Mexico
City, Lima, Bogotá, Rio de Janeiro and Buenos Aires), the
stolid, phlegmatic-appearing mestizo has begun to learn to
smile, even laugh, and to believe that he has some rights. He
has not yet learned to fight for these rights or even how to
exercise them, but he knows that they exist and, theoretically,
that they are his. The pelado or mestizo of each country shares
more similarities than there exist differences.

The Mexican revolution became a social revolution and it
is to be distinguished from other Ibero-American revolutions
that occur with a certain degree of regularity. In the latter, the
uprisings are either palace coups or they result from the
intervention of the military. In Spanish, the former are *golpe
de estado,* and the latter *cuartelazo,* literally, "a blow from the
barracks." The coups and overthrowals are for achieving

power while giving lip service to reform, egalitarianism, and the breakup of *latifundia,* large landholdings. In a few, e.g. Mexico, Peru, and Chile, there has been a substantial distribution of land to the peasants or *campesinos.*

Ezequiel Martínez Estrada wrote in his book, *Diferéncias y Semejanzas Entre Los Paises de la America Latina,* "Differences and Similarities Among the Latin American Nations" (42:18, 19),

> Latin America has not attained, and obstinately refuses to propose for itself an outline of its own civilization and its complete dependence on physical roots from Africa, and culture from Europe. [Latin America] will not face up to the fact that its sources make of her an immense conglomeration of heterogeneities. She has a plasticity which makes her susceptible to the influx of every class of social modality. In addition to being permeable, she is fragile and a vassal to the pressure and forces that may be exerted upon her. If, of the North Americas, we can say that it is a cosmopolitan conglomeration fused in a solid state of action and thought, then, of Latin America, we can say that it is a combination of many racial and nationalistic mixtures whose elements have not yet set.

Martínez Estrada adds that environmental and other forces maintain a state of tension and conflict with the distinct forms which labor to perpetuate themselves. He comments on the differentiated and disintegrated body of Latin America whose cohesiveness has been attained by outer coercion, which is the tragic political drama of Hispano-America.

Martínez Estrada's reference to "an immense conglomeration of heterogeneities" requires some amplification. Michael D. Olien in his *Latin Americans: Contemporary Peoples and Their Tradition* (45A:132–139) discusses at length the various groups of European and Far Eastern peoples who have populated Latin America since the middle of the nineteenth century. There are large Chinese populations in Cuba, Peru, Mexico and Jamaica. Almost 65 percent of the restaurants (excluding luxury hotel dining rooms) in Lima and Callao, Peru, are owned and operated by Chinese and Japanese. While the Chinese population of the nations in which they are to be found may not be large numerically, their economic importance is "far beyond their numerical importance."

There are large enclaves of Middle Eastern peoples in Argentina, Mexico and most of the Central American countries. These people, regardless of their national origins, are usually called *Turcos*, Turks. The Lebanese and Syrians predominate. Among these *Turcos* are almost 300,000 Jews. The others are either Christian (especially the Lebanese) or Moslems. The Moslems predominate in Argentina, Surinam and Guatemala. There are many East Indians in the Guianas and some of the Caribbean islands. The present Javanese population of Surinam is estimated at 43,000.

Many other religious sects have formed religious colonies and contribute to the heterogeneity. There are several thousand Mennonites in northern Mexico, northeast Brazil, Paraguay and Bolivia; Quakers in Mexico; and almost one million Jews throughout Latin America. Argentina has the largest number, 450,000; Brazil about 165,000; Mexico 50,000; Chile about 30,000; Peru about 30,000; and the rest are to be found scattered in each of the other countries.

4 ● Machismo and Sex

The mestizo is the progenitor of what is called the cult of *machismo*. *Macho* is the word for the male who enacts machismo. The Mexican psychiatrist Dr. Jorge Segura Millán delivered a lecture on machismo and it was reported almost at length in *Novedades'* Cultural Section of May 22, 1966. At the outset, Dr. Millán stated that machismo was a show-off or ostentatious person's boasting of his valor. He added that machismo nourishes itself in the blood and marrow (he used the Spanish word *savia*—"sap") and daily renews the Mexican male in his way of life. He traced the sources of machismo to the Spanish conquistador, a paradigm of masculinity, who burned with lust and who sexually possessed the female autochthonous. This, as we have indicated, created a new race, the mestizo, who was not incubated in the warmth of love. The violated woman was disowned by her own people.

He concluded his lecture with this definition: machismo is the attitude adopted by Mexicans as a role for life and is based on the inferiority complex manifested extrovertedly as superiority, principally in sexual affairs accompanied by aggressiveness and sado-masochism.

Because the mestizo is unsure of his loudly proclaimed virility, he supports, through machismo, the image he hopes to reflect of himself as macho. (Cubans deride the term and mock it as a sign of the puerility of Mexicans and Central Americans.) Machismo being the cult of virility, it is compared often to the he-goat in human form who rules and violates. (In Spanish, the verb is *chingar*.) Machismo and *chingar* are closely related. The verb is used commonly by the people in the lower economic classes—the servile and subjugated peoples who require an emotional and verbal catharsis. *Chingar* is used as an expletive and as an obscenity although it has other meanings, e.g., "idea of failure," or in Colombia, "to be disappointed," or "to be made a fool of." Words derived from *chingar* are epithets.

The macho is *el gran chingon*. Macho represents power. *La chingada* is defined by Paz as "one of the Mexican representatives of Maternity" (47:75) and as "the mother forcibly opened, violated, or deceived; but a mythical mother—not real" (24:29). *El hijo de la chingada*, "the son of the mother violated or deceived," is therefore the offspring of rape, abduction, seduction, or other form of deceit. It is noteworthy that, in Mexico, mestizos when moved by fury, excess euphoria, extreme frustration, or sheer enthusiasm will shout, *"Vivá Mexico, hijos de la chingada."*

The mestiza and Indian female do not use birth control pills or any contraceptive device. Nor does the male. He desires to have a woman conceive because that is proof of his virility. Women refrain from doing anything to defeat the fulfillment of the male desire and therefore they desist from any birth control measures. Latin American courts do not order fathers to support bastards or "natural" children. Support for *licit*, legitimate, children will be directed more often than the payment of alimony to the legal wife and, if it be ordered, alimony is only for a limited period.

Machismo is also reflected in some of the child-mother relationships. Despite living proof to the contrary, many women continue to believe that a child at the breast acts as a bar

to conception. The mestiza and Indian female breed prolifi-
cally. While a year-old child will be sucking at her breast, she
will be bearing another. (Her husband or man, having had
proof of his virility, is not insistent on more children, especially if he supports his family and has limited means.) The
mother who must continue her role as wife without any
abatement of any duties can shower her attention and visible
affection only on the youngest of her offspring. With the
arrival of a new child, maternal care and attention is diverted
to that one. The older female siblings become substitute
mothers to the younger ones. The male sibling does nothing to
relieve the mother's household duties.

It is touching and memorable to see a four- or five-year-
old girl carrying her one- or two-year-old brother or sister in
her *rebozo*, shawl, or leading the toddler by the hand down the
street.

Boys learn at an early age to help with male work. They
enjoy the preferred male status. Some Latin American anthropologists believe that the breaking of the piñata on Christmas
is symbolic of the resentment felt through displacement from
the mother's *rebozo* by the arrival of the next child. The
blindfolded child with the stick who attempts to break the
suspended papier-mâché animal or *olla*, clay pot, is really
seeking, symbolically, to revenge himself on the enlarged
stomach of his mother because from it came the child who
displaced him from her attentions and breasts and started him
on the road to the adult role and responsibility he was forced to
assume before he learned to play. The young male may openly
resent his mother during adolescence. He is then free of her
apron strings and commands. This exhibition of resentment
is denied to the female.

The macho is aggressive and insensitive. While *macho*
and *pelado*, "plucked and hairless," are not synonymous
terms, they have much in common. Machismo crosses all
strata of society, while the *pelado* is limited to the lower
classes. Erico Verissimo, a Brazilian, uses *macho* and *pelado*
synonymously. He describes the characteristics of ". . . his

false pride, his desire to appear what he is not, to impose himself, his capacity for simulation and the abundance of sexual allusion in the terminology of the pelado" (67:333). In Brazil, the gaucho of Rio Grande de Sul has an identical tendency. Ramos attributes the custom of casting doubts on the masculinity of the opponent in heated arguments to the lack of this quality in the accuser. Possibly the custom of eating dried bull's testicles (a delicacy in some rural areas) represents an attempt to achieve a virility which nature has denied him. It is possible that this belief stemmed from earlier Indian customs.

In pre-Columbian days, the pagan priests of the Aztecs would tear still-beating hearts from the breasts of captured foreign warriors. The hearts and the blood were offered as food to the Sun god. The cadaver of the warrior was thrown down the temple steps. The crowd below would grab an arm or a thigh of one of the cadavers and eat the flesh. The raw human flesh was not consumed as food. The people believed that some of the courage and virility of the deceased warrior—only the brave were offered as sacrifices—would be acquired by the consumption of his flesh. This was not an act of cannibalism.

In the eighteenth century, Abbé Reynal, a Frenchman, wrote a history of the New World. He attributed the ease of the Spanish conquest to the sexual virility of the Spaniards which attracted the Indian women who had known only the Indian bedmates as weak and ineffectually satisfying partners. This aspersion on the Indians' ability in lectual combat was repeated in the twentieth century by the sentence, "Latins are lousy lovers."

The Latin American who walks with his arm resting on the shoulder of his female companion does so because he is emphasizing his virility. He is impressing, mentally and physically, upon the young lady that he is masculine and that some degree of possession is involved in their relationship. The cult of the male is reflected throughout the society in such customs as the salutation in letters to a married couple. The envelope is addressed to "Sr. Juan Garcia y la Sra." (Mr. John

Garcia and his wife.) The letter will start "Dear Juan and Maria."

To the macho, every woman is fair prey. However, the females of his family are sacrosanct and are to be defended from lewdness, obscenity and advances of other males. The macho wants his bride to be a virgin. Surveys have shown that Latin couples indulge in less frequent sexual relations than their American counterparts. Wives are for child bearing, and mistresses for sexual divertissements. The qualifications on the foregoing statement are that they are generalizations for machismo. Divorce is becoming socially acceptable.

Divorce proceedings are usually instituted by the male. The courts are prone to apply masculine justice, but the growth in the number of divorce suits initiated by women is symptomatic of a liberation of the female and a weakening of the male position as family autocrat.

Homosexuality is common and is not regarded with the puritanical disdain of Anglo-Saxons. It was an old Spanish, as well as an old Indian, custom. There were many cases before the various tribunals of the Inquisition in New Spain, Cartagena, Lima, and Santiago de Chile of sodomy between priests or monks and young boys. This practice by the clergy was considered only mildly immoral, but yet subject to trial. Its occurrence was a result of preference rather than the lack of opportunity to enjoy the sexual pleasures of the opposite sex.

The archives of the Inquisition Tribunals in Mexico, Cartagena, Peru, Buenos Aires and the Archivo Historico Nacional de Madrid, which have many of the *procesos*, minutes of trial proceedings recorded almost like modern trial proceedings, from the New World, also reveal the practice of the solicitation of women for sexual intercourse by priests and monks in the confessional and other places. The name of the offense that appears most frequently is *"por solicitante de sus hijas espirituales,"* "for solicitation of his spiritual daughters." So frequent was the crime that the Suprema of the Inquisition in Spain ruled that the crime existed only when the solicitation took place while the confessor was in the confession box. The records indicate that confessions were interrupted when the spiritual father hearing the confession felt the call of carnal desire. He then adjourned the hearing of the confession. He and the woman went to his private quarters where he suggested that the devil be exorcised from the body of the confessor by copulation. Eca de Queiroz advances the clerical justification for such conduct in the English translation of his excellent novel, *The Sin of Father Amaro.*

Former United States Senator Ernest Gruening's book, *Mexico and Its Heritage,* is based upon his experiences in Mexico and the research he did there. He reports the story of a priest who was assigned to a parish in the back country, which included an Indian village. When he made his first visit to this village, the Indians, having been foretold of his arrival, met him at the border of the village led by their chiefs and three beautiful maidens. He was then informed by the chiefs that the girls were being presented to him for the fulfillment of his desires. He, in return for this gift, was requested not to sexually molest the wives, daughters and sisters of the inhabitants of the village. It was reported by Stuart Chase in his book, *Mexico,* that a monk is said to have sired thirty children by seven mothers. These incidents, which are representative of many, indicate that until recent decades the clergy with heterosexual inclinations did not have to repress themselves (8:104).

Of course, there were innumerable others to whom the vow of celibacy was sacred. There were some who interpreted the vow to apply only to relations with females and not to males, especially young ones. This inclination was also found among the Indians. Mariano Picón Salas quotes from *The True History of the Conquest of New Spain,* in which the author, Bernal Díaz del Castillo, reports on "certain sexual habits of the Aztecs which were much too Greek" (25:23). (The Greeks had the word for it.)

There is a private museum in Lima which houses a collection of Inca ceramic objects decorated with figures engaged in the gamut of sexual expression, from aberration to transvestites. All are displayed on jugs and vases that were also functional. Inca civilization may not have produced an alphabet, the wheel, or literature, but in its ceramic arts it revealed its complete and thorough knowledge of all varieties of sexual activity.

Pure homosexuality, male or female, is not common in Latin America. The cult of machismo may be one of the factors militating against total abstinence from sexual relations with the opposite sex. There are many who indulge in heterosexual relationships but for whom homosexuality is the stronger urge. It is not rare for such men to be married and the father, usually, of one child. However, their preference for male companionship is well known. (Lesbianism is most rare.) Some such men have held high offices in various countries. Sex in Latin America is considered a very personal affair. The rule would appear to be that whatever any two adult people do privately and without damage to society is their own affair.

Machismo has nothing spartan-like about it. It is not necessary to be really brave or strong. Machismo evidences itself in verbalisms, in the carrying of a gun or switch blade, and in the exercise of power. (The exercise of power is discussed below.) This may explain in part why so often the Ibero-Americans will say "yes" when they mean "no," and why *mañana* may mean tomorrow to the listener, when the speaker mentally and deliberately chooses to interpret it as the indefinite future. It is part of their fantasy playing and it gives them an opportunity to deceive the person with whom they are dealing, thereby keeping themselves in control of a situation. To many, it is part of a power ploy.

The small shopkeeper and artisan will willingly promise to have something made or ready at a particular time. He knows that it cannot be finished within the allotted time, but he still says, "Yes, I'll have it for you." How does he resolve this? Dr. Díaz Guerrero, the Mexican psychiatrist, offered the following explanation which, he said, were the thoughts of the shopkeeper or artisan:

1. The promiser may die before the time promised and thus be relieved of the obligation.

2. The recipient of the promise may die and thus not require fulfillment of the promise.

3. The customer may renege on the contract and thus end the transaction.

4. Others whose work had priority may cancel their orders and thereby fulfillment may be possible.

5. The promisee may wait to inquire until the day following the day promised for delivery. This allows for an extra day. An explanation of sickness or emergency can absolve the delay and a new date can be promised.

6. *Quién sabe,* who knows? A miracle may occur and the work can be completed.

During the time between the making of the promise and the due date, the customer was happy. Made happy by whom? He or she was made happy by the artisan or storeowner who, by ·agreeing amicably to the date requested, made the other happy. To make people happy is an exercise of power. There is also the counterpart: once the promiser has the job or contract, together with a deposit, all is dependent upon him. This is also power. Latins are not litigious since they are cynical about justice and their courts. Latins do not walk out in a huff on the first breach because that is an admission of weakness. So the game of power is played and there are many ploys.

The female breast is sacrosanct to the mestiza. She would not imprison her buttocks in a girdle, but her breasts have to be encased as tightly as possible. The Mexican, Cuban and Central American male regards a woman's buttocks as a more important criterion of female pulchritude than the mammary glands. It was a Latin custom to pinch the derrieres of attractive women as late as the 1950s. Mexico City passed an ordinance making pinching illegal because female tourists took umbrage when they were the objects. The act of pinching to the male was equivalent to the American whistle. In several countries, falsies for the buttocks enjoy a greater sale than falsies for the flat-chested woman in this country. Except in the most cosmopolitan of the social strata where the influence of foreign standards prevails, young women tighten the lower half of their skirts so that they cup and accentuate the contour of the rear. The absence of a girdle permits a woman to sway suggestively as she walks. In the past few years one has begun to see the Latin American version of the sweater girl and the mini-skirt in the cities. Hot pants and mini-skirts are the vogue for the liberated Latin working girl. American and other foreign films have aided greatly in refocusing the eyes and attention of the males.

Sometimes women exercise machismo, although one would never say to or about a woman, *muy macha* or *qué macha*, "what a woman!" The female is prohibited from the open exercise of male-like power. One sees a brand of "female machismo" practiced by the lower classes in the cities. In the supermarkets and large stores, the cashier will act disdainfully to the *muchacha*, the servant girl, especially if it is evident that she is a new arrival from the country. If the purchase is small, the cashier will not put it into a bag even if it is a bottle of milk or a pound of butter. If change is to be made, the cashier will make it in the smallest coin denomination. This may be explained in American terms by giving a dollar for a ten cent item and receiving ninety pennies in change.

The holding back of a paper bag, or the dumping of many coins, is an exercise of power. In this instance, the cashier will do this only to someone whom she regards as her inferior, and who is too timorous to complain. Similar incidents and indignities may be observed as one climbs the social ladder or the ladder of power. Members of each level of society attempt to exercise power over those of lower levels. It is a form of social segregation.

While racial segregation is almost nonexistent in Latin America, social stratification and segregation exist in most of the countries. Vertical social mobility is almost nonexistent. Class lines are rigid except that one can move from the very poor to the middle class as one's income improves. This is a reflection of power.

As previously stated, the mestizo constitutes the largest single group in all Latin America. He is a new "race," and, consequently, he and those who sympathize with him rightfully request tolerance and understanding. He is the product of interbreeding and cross-fertilization of many races: black, red, white, and yellow. He has been surrounded by multiple ethnic influences and is the confused product of all of them.

There is a turbulence within him. The infusion of genes and chromosomes of disparate sources, while not creating a new race in an anthropological or genetic sense, does produce a new man. This man is just awakening and he is still in a transitional stage. His volatility is understandable. He has no firm roots except in a soil that he is just beginning to claim as his own.

Many of his actions are reactions and defensive. He does not initiate courses of action but rather responds to external stimuli. He is not open enough to love. His hates, which are intense, are usually predicated upon fear and distrust. Being insecure, he adopts as his elementary rule of thumb a distrust of all that is strange or foreign. While he may not actively repel, he seeks to avoid contact with anything beyond the familiar and his immediate circle.

A Freudian would say that he seeks a return to the foetal stage so as to hide within the womb. He feels that he was rejected by the womb, and this may account for his attitude toward the female. Machismo may be compensatory.

He also hates, because for centuries he was nurtured on the bitter aloes of frustration, denial, contempt, maltreatment, and scorn. He tasted these things in his mother's milk. They were lashed into his body by the cold that penetrated his shoddy, beggarly clothes. They were etched in his mind by what he saw happening to his mother and his sisters, and by the contempt showered on his father. Geneticists to the contrary notwithstanding, there must be an emotional heredity. The emotional heritage is the soil from which springs the mestizo character of today.

The emerging liberated Latin American woman has begun to show disrespect for machos and their cult. The double standard is slowly being whittled away. The independent woman contends that machos are infantile men whose boasts of sexual prowess are empty words, whose virility is verbal only. The cult of machismo is indicative of instability in the institutions of home and government because it is a bar to cooperation and equality among men. Machos are poor sports and don't know how to be "good losers." As Georgie Anne Geyer wrote, "They can be charming . . . perhaps worst of all, they are men who are incapable of creating modern societies" (19:103).

5 ● Religion

If any part of Latin America is uniquely Spanish, it is the Catholic Church. Catholicism in the Western World is divided into two branches: Roman Catholicism and Spanish Catholicism. Ever since 1506 when Pope Alexander VI granted King Ferdinand the *patronato real*—literally "the royal patronage"—the right to name all the Church hierarchy in the New World, to collect all the tithes, create dioceses, and so forth in return for the royal promise to support the Church, the Spanish clergy owed their principal allegiance to the king. No papal bull, encyclical, or edict could be read unless the king authorized the reading and the publication thereof.

In 1904, Angel F. de Ganivet wrote, "Spain was the nation which created a Christianity that was most its own" (16:13). During the colonial period, the secular clergy, the parish priest, was limited to whites and to serving the white society. The nonwhites were served by the monastic orders. This decision resulted in inter-clerical dissension. Charles Gibson wrote, "Church history in colonial Spanish America is a history of constant internal squabbles" (20:78).

José Miguez Bonino, an Argentine theologian, wrote a few years ago, "Christianity never took root as such in Latin America. Latin America was never Christian in the sense that Europe or even North America can be said to be so. What took place here was a colossal transplantation—the basic ecclesiastical structures, disciplines, and ministries were brought wholesale from Spain . . . a tremendous form without substance. Is it strange that the continent which numbers a third of the whole Roman communion has not produced a single outstanding theologian, or an important order, and very few saints?" Robert Wood, S.M., has admitted the Catholic "conversion" of Latin America in terms of cultural syncretism or as a religious veneer with little real meaning (cf. 83:2).

Even in the Church—a place that should offer solace and comfort at least to the spirit—the Latin American is confronted with suffering, blood, tears, and desecration. Churches in no other parts of the world have as many statues of the martyred Jesus with his crown of thorns as do those in Latin America. Most churches were built during colonial times. It is a rarity to see Jesus in repose and as part of the Godhead. The visual, physical reproductions of Jesus portray him with a bowed head, the spear of the Roman soldier in his side, the blood flowing from the open wounds on the body, a malaise and sadness of visage that must cause an involuntary resentment in the untutored devout onlooker against those whom he thinks caused this. W. Stanley Rycroft wrote, "The Spanish Christ is a tragic victim. In Spain, as in Latin America, can be seen the bruised, livid and blood-streaked images of Christ. One gains a deeper understanding of the contrast between the living, risen, eternal Christ and the dead Christ of Latin America by visiting the shrine on top of Montserrate Hill overlooking Bogotá" (57:118).

Even the *posada*,* holy pilgrimage before Christmas each year, is a reenactment of the rejection by man of Jesus and, by transference, this appears to the mestizo to be a rejection of

---

*Posada also means an inn.

himself. The *posada* has many forms, but the one that is acted out in many places in Latin America in December (sometimes each night for a week or more prior to Christmas) is the parade in which Mary and Joseph are depicted seeking refuge at various doors and being refused admittance. Each parade ends at the doors of a church; the doors finally open and the procession is welcomed. The symbolism of the parade, the doleful music sung and played during the march, are annual reminders to the Indians and mestizos that they, as were Mary and Joseph, are refused by all, that their entrance is barred, and that it is their fate to be met by cruelty, denial, and rejection. The final hospitality of the Church consists of a superstition-centered, blind, pseudo-Christianity in which solace of a kind is found. It is difficult to hope for an improved existence in this life since the priest, the instrument of the Church, often lives but little better than his poor parishioners.

The mother of Jesus almost always has tears on her cheeks. As the Virgin of Guadalupe, she is the most important patron saint in most of Latin America by virtue of the immense area in which she is adored and the number of her adherents. She is the "Brown Virgin." Because she is *morena*, brown, and because she is identified with Latin America, she is uniquely the mestizo's. The story goes that she appeared to an Indian, Juan Diego, in 1531 while he was walking over a hill on the outskirts of Mexico City. Coincidentally this hill was the home of the mother of the Indian gods, who also had an immaculate conception as a result of a feather falling from heaven on her stomach. The Catholic Virgin appeared three times to Juan Diego. On her last appearance, she performed a miracle by making roses appear in his apron. Bishop Juan de Zumárraga, to whom Juan had reported the two prior visions, had refused to believe the Indian's tale. After the appearance of the roses, it is said that the Bishop believed that a miracle had occurred and ordered the shrine of Guadalupe erected on the site.

It may be because of the foregoing that the cult of Marianna has assumed major importance. The cult is also known as Maryology and has made of the Holy Trinity a Quartet. Mestizos do not pray to Mary to intercede with Her son as is the custom in most places. The Virgin of Guadalupe is considered a part of the Godhead and prayers are addressed to Her on the virtue of Her own authority. She is co-equal and has been deified. More often than not, she is shown without the Child. This cult of Maryology or Marianna is of concern to the Roman Catholic Church and was discussed at the Vatican Council in 1963.

John A. Mackay wrote *The Other Spanish Christ* and attributed the situation to these causes:

> A Christ known in life as an infant, and in death as a corpse, over whose helpless childhood the Virgin Mother presides; . . . who, by not tasting death became the Queen of life—that is the Christ and Virgin who came to America! He came as Lord of Death . . . she came as a sovereign lady of life."

The Creole Christ, said Mackay, has another aspect, "his lack of humanity," which is attributable to the lack of knowledge of Jesus. He continues, "This is one reason why Christ is not considered in the role of a mediator and why the intercession of Mary and of the saints is given such importance" (37:95).

Innumerable towns throughout Latin America have their own local patron saint. The names of most of them begin with "The Virgin. . ." or "Our Lady of. . . ." Cuba's patron saint is la Nuestra Señora de la Caridad del Cobre. *(Cobre* means "copper" but it is also the name of a town in Cuba.) Santa Barbara, another "virgin" in Cuba, is considered a transference of the African Negro god, Changó, brought to Cuba by the Negroes. Venezuela's patron saint is La Virgen de Corcomato.

Representatives of the Virgin of Guadalupe often show that she has a dark skin, almost black. However, when she is holding the baby Jesus in her arms, the baby's face is white.

The strength and support of the Church is among the women. A possible explanation for the elevation of Mary may lie in the role of the woman in the family life and the comparison that she makes between herself and the Holy Mother. Mary was long-suffering; she endured the pain and grief of observing the trials and tribulations of Her son, whom she never doubted nor abandoned. The Latin American female and Mary have much in common, and consequently, the Church's disciples feel that Mary can empathize with them while Jesus is a male and aloof to the burdens of women.

David Riesman, in *The Lonely Crowd*, divided societies into tradition-directed, inner-directed, and other-directed (56:8). The last category is not present in Latin America to any great extent. Urban mestizos are in a transition process from tradition- to inner-directed in the secular aspects of their lives. With respect to religion or the spiritual phase of the lives of most Latin Americans, however, including the mestizos and the Indians, we find that, with the exception of the cultured and the cosmopolites of the oligarchy, tradition-directed is the most apt description.

The formal rituals of Catholicism as practiced in Latin America are an adjunct of religious practice of tradition-directed societies. The high degree of illiteracy of the masses is a factor in encouraging and valuing the pageantry and extreme formalism of the Church. The practices stress form, not substance. Stanley Rycroft commented that "lack of an ethic in Spanish religion constitutes its problem, as it constitutes the problem of the religion transplanted in the New World." (This quote was taken by Rycroft from *The Invisible Christ* by Ricardo Rojas, pp. 83-84.)

The Church in the colonial Spanish empire was responsible to the king of Spain, not to the pope. Of the thirty archbishops of Mexico (1535-1821), ten became viceroys and held similar high offices in South America. The relationships between priests and people were close (spiritually and physically) and still are in rural areas. The peccadillos of some priests or monks may have caused some parishioners to lose confidence in the sanctity of their spiritual fathers and others may have disapproved of the abuses of the Church in amassing great wealth and lending money at exorbitant rates of interest (45A:76), but the masses distinguished between faith *qua* faith and the institutions and people dispensing the sacraments of the faith.

Padre Miguel Hidalgo y Costilla, an ordained priest, is not only considered the father of his country, but is also the paternal ancestor of living people. As late as 1961, two of his great-great-granddaughters were receiving pensions from the Mexican government because they were his descendants.

The Catholic priests were excellent showmen. The poor and the downtrodden could look without envy upon the riches of the House of the Lord. Their unpaid days, weeks, and months of toil and their paltry centavos were willingly granted for the erection of cathedrals and churches. These were considered way stations on the road to the glorious Paradise that awaited them in the world hereafter.

The Indian, the mestizo, and the Latin American poor in general seek solace and comfort in religion. The abstract is beyond their comprehension, especially when it involves faith and theology. The wooden images, the glass in front of a statue of the Virgin, the bleeding of Jesus, the somber carvings and paintings of innumerable saints are holy in themselves. They are not representations or symbolic. They (the figures) *are* the granters of blessings.

The formalized institutions of a culture make any change difficult. One of the reasons ascribed for the comparative ease of the Spanish conquest of the New World is that Spaniards fought to kill; by killing they hoped to inspire fear among the Indians. The Indians fought to take prisoners either to be offered as sacrifices to the gods, as did the Aztecs, or as slaves, as did some South American tribes. The Aztecs never attacked at night and fought according to formal rules that were unknown to the Spaniards or were deliberately disregarded because they knew that by such actions they threw their Indian adversaries off guard and into confusion.*

The formal rules also serve as a defense for tradition–di-

---

*Magnus Mörner writes, "In a way, the Spanish conquest . . . was a conquest of women. The Spaniards obtained the Indian girls both by force and by peaceful means" (43:22).

rected peoples and a bulwark against change. By hewing to the rigid patterns of formalized action, there is acceptance and approval by the group and by one's peers, and life presents no problems. Only the deviant is confronted by trouble.

The republics of Latin America are considered to be Catholic countries because the majority of the populations of each of them profess Catholicism. Stress must be laid on the word "profess," which is distinguished from practice. Freedom of conscience or freedom of religion is guaranteed under all the constitutions, although in Costa Rica, Venezuela, Colombia, and Argentina, Catholicism is either the state religion or receives a special subsidy.

Mexico and Uruguay are at the other end of the spectrum. In Uruguay, Christmas is officially designated as "Family Day," Easter week as "Tourist Week," and Epiphany (January 6) as "Children's Day." In Mexico the legal rights of the clergy are minimal. They may not hold public office. No religious garb may be worn in public by the clergy or religious representatives of either sex of any faith. (Those seen in the streets in clerical or nun's attire are usually visitors.) No church, regardless of sect or denomination, is allowed to own property. All church property was expropriated under the 1857 Laws of Reform. All temples, churches, and synagogues and any other buildings used for purposes of prayer belong to the State.

If a new house of worship is to be erected, a deed to the land is given to the government's Secretaria Patrimonia Nacional. When the building is completed, the government gives the sponsoring organization a ninety-nine-year lease at a nominal rental of $1.00 per year, and all future repairs and alterations must be made by the organization. The exception to this rule was made in 1966 when the Cathedral in Mexico City was severely damaged by fire. The government agreed to bear part of the cost of repairs because the Cathedral is a leading tourist attraction. This act of cooperation is part of the modus vivendi that has been established between the government and the Church since President Avila Gamacho dared to say in 1940, "I am a believer," *soy un creyente*.

Mexican clergymen are barred from holding office and from making any political partisan appeals from their pulpits. It is an open secret that the Church would prefer to see PAN, the Partido Acción Nacional, in power instead of PRI. The latter has never lost a national election. While parochial schools exist as private schools licensed by the Secretaria de Educación, they are barred from teaching religion. The regulation applies to all faiths. The rule, however, has been observed more in the breach, especially in the last few years, because custom, ceremonies, and religious history are taught in addition to the government-prescribed secular courses. Dogma, creed, and theology are omitted. Only ten hours a week are permitted for extracurricular studies of any kind in all private schools. Anything other than the State-prescribed curriculum is extracurricular. This creates a problem for Jewish schools, which exist in order to teach Hebrew and Yiddish in addition to other subjects pertaining to Jewish culture, such as literature, history, and music.

The faculties and courses of the private schools are prescribed, since all secular studies must follow the curriculum set forth by the Ministry of Education and must be taught by its licensed teachers. The ministry submits the names of the teachers licensed by the Ministry of Education. Salaries are paid for by each school. As a generalization for all Latin America, it may be said that there exists an anticlerical attitude, but not one that is antireligious. At worst, the institutions are feared, not the faith.

Spanish clergymen in the Americas were noted for their illiteracy, venality, and partiality to the wealthy. This is not to deny that there were pious monks. There were God-inspired priests and regular and secular clergy who sought to aid the poor, the oppressed, and the heathen and who strove to inculcate and indoctrinate the lessons of the Church.

In 1767 Charles III expelled the Jesuits from Spain and its empire because he feared their power in the Americas, their influence among the Indians, and their Pious Fund, which had become a major banking institution. The Pious Fund was financing the Philippine galleons, faring between the Far East and Acapulco and Lima, and collecting interest ranging as high as 1,000 percent. One of the legacies that the Jesuits bequeathed to the New World was the doctrine that the end justifies the means. This tenet has been incorporated into every phase of Latin American life. The Jesuits, however, did more to advance learning than other segments of the Church.

When the New World colonies broke loose from the mother country, Spain, in the first two decades of the nineteenth century, the Holy See at first refused to recognize the new nations. Even after recognition, a dispute continued to rage over the power of ecclesiastical appointments. The new nations contended that the rights of the *patronato real* passed to them as successors of the crown, while Rome contended that the rights were personal to the kings of Spain and reverted to Rome upon independence from Spain. In addition to this controversy, there has been the continuing struggle for the control over education, marriage ceremonies, and minority sects. This last question has been disposed of in favor of minorities, but, as Thomas Jefferson said, "Eternal vigilance is the price of liberty."

Minority sects must remain on the *que vive* as long as there is a strong conservative, old guard, powerful group among the Latin American clergy. In 1962, a canon of the Cathedral in Mexico City called for revival of the Inquisition, not only against the Jews, but also against liberal Catholic leaders such as the then Archbishop Mirando and Bishop Sergio Méndez of Cuernavaca.

The Indian "reconquest" is evident in the interpretation given to much of the Catholic symbolism and ritual. In many respects the Indians are proof of a statement made in the sixteenth century by the Spaniard, Luis Vives, that Christianity goes on, but it does not necessarily make Christians of its adherents. The Indians and mestizos of the lower economic classes in Guatemala, Nicaragua, Colombia, Ecuador, Bolivia, Chile, and Brazil may profess Christianity, but their practices and beliefs reflect their pagan ancestry and the enduring qualities of the original faith. J. Lloyd Mecham, in his *Church and State in Latin America,* observed that "practicing Catholics . . . come to between 15 and 30 percent of the entire population." The question that was put to a Latin American, "What is your religion?" and to which he answered, "I am an atheist, thank God," may be a jest, but there is more truth than humor in the reply. It must be made clear, however, that religion is a most serious matter even to those who profess none. There are activists on both sides. In the states of Nuevo León and Tamaulipas in Mexico and in parts of Colombia and Peru, there are annual incidents of assassinations of Protestants and other non-Catholics.

Animosity between Catholics and Protestants is revealed by the doctoral dissertation of Maria Cassareto for the Mexican National University on the history of Mexican Protestantism in the nineteenth and twentieth centuries. She shows that in many rural areas, Protestants do not reveal their faith to the census-taker. Fear causes them to assert that they are Catholics. This is borne out by the discrepancy in the Mexican decennial census of 1960 which showed that there are 595,000 Protestants in the country, but the renowned demographer, the Jesuit Rivero R., in his book published in 1961 gives a figure in excess of 1,200,000 Protestants in the nation.

While traditional Protestant churches have not made rapid progress in most Latin American states, the Pentecostals have made the greatest advances. The Professors Wiarda wrote that ". . . there is an egalitarianism among the Pentecostals that is lacking in the older churches [in Brazil], both Protestant and Catholic. . . . Protestantism has met with little success because it fails to reach the grass roots and to come to grips with the complex social problems." In several places there is a Catholic revival due to a reinvigorated lay movement and the influx of young priests with concepts of social justice learned in America, Belgium, Holland, and even Germany. Using the poverty-ridden northeast of Brazil as an example, we quote from the Wiardas' article that "a corps of radically reform-oriented priests began to organize the peasantry, urge dialogue with the Marxists, and talk of revolutionary changes to come." These last are prophetic words, not only for Brazil, but for several other Latin military dictatorships who talk of justice, but fail to act.

When this author was engaged in writing the history of the Jews of New Spain* (University of Miami Press, 1970), I went to the Mexican state of Chiapas, which borders Guatemala, and spent several days with the late Franz Blom and his wife. Blom was formerly director of the Middle American Institute of Tulane University, had resided in and about San Cristobal de las Casas (second largest city in Chiapas) for almost forty years, and knew the southern portion of Mexico and northern Guatemala better than any other person. The 1940 government decennial census reported an "Israelita" population of 483 in Chiapas, one of Mexico's least developed states, and one in which almost 80 percent of the vast Indian population neither spoke nor understood Spanish. For 1950, the "Israelita" population has been decreased to 300 and by 1960 to 183. Why had Jews gone there in the first instance? Why had so many left in a span of ten years? These were two of the several questions that puzzled this writer.

A Jew in Tuxtla Gutierrez, capital of the state of Chiapas, was interviewed prior to ascending the mountain to San Cristobal. The Jew stated that there were only thirty-two Jews in the entire state, and that there never had been 183, much less 483. He had no explanation for the official figures. Blom, however, had a ready explanation. The census-takers are drafted and serve without pay. They are recommended by the leading political figure. Since the Church was very influential in the cities of Chiapas, the census-takers were devout Catholics. Catholics prefer Judaism to Protestantism because the former has no missionaries and does not proselytize. Consequently, when some interviewees stated their religion to be *Protestante,* the census-takers would ignore the reply and place him in the category *Israelita,* a synonym for Jew. Blom

---

*New Spain was the name of the Spanish viceroyalty which included Mexico, Central America, the Philippines and what is now Southwest U.S.A.

completed the explanation with the remark anent the number of Jews in Chiapas, "This was the largest complimentary vote that the Jews ever received."

Prior to the advent of the Spanish conquistadors, religion was highly exalted among the natives. The conquistadors were accompanied by clergy, and while the cross may not have held first place in practice, it was part of the threefold motivation for conquest, "God, gold, and greed." The kind of Catholicism that took root was not that postulated by the Vatican. Samuel Ramos held that it was most difficult for Indians to adopt Catholicism because there is no vocabulary for an abstract God or dogma in the Indian tongues (55:74).

The grandeur of Church architecture was caused by the Spanish desire to surpass the splendor of the pagan pyramids and temples. There is an interweaving of the old paganism with the strong Spanish Catholicism. Catholicism did implant the seeds of the classicist mind on the American continents. It was this fertilization that permitted the transplantation of the baroque and Churiqueresque French and Spanish cultures until the early decades of the twentieth century.

Latin Americans have been going through a transitional period in religion and culture. For almost two centuries, they have been imitative. In order to wean themselves from foreign influences, as well as for other cogent reasons, they sought to throw off the shackles of religion. Chile's largest single political party, the Radical, is professedly anticlerical and freethinking. While certain men are for complete cleavage between Church and State, there are liberals such as the former Chilean President Eduardo Frei Montalva, a Christian Democrat, who believe that Christianity can supply the inspiration to work for the common good for the majority of the people. Frei was proven wrong by the 1970 elections which brought Salvador Allende, a Marxist, to the presidency. The present military junta under President General Pinochet subscribes to the Christian ethic but gives the junta's concept of the people's needs the highest priority.

In 1960, the Mexican Church felt it might publicly voice

its belief that Christian social justice, as laid down by the Catholic Church, was necessary as a prop against the encroachment of communism. The Church openly criticized Partido de la Revolucion Institucion (the major and most powerful political party) for its insufficient concern with social justice. PRI permitted some of its people to suggest publicly that the time may have come to again place the clergy in jail. (This reference was to the War of the Cristeros, 1926-1929.)

The major battles in Latin America between the Church and State from the time of independence until the present have been over control of education, marriage and divorce, disposition of Church property, and the tolerance of dissenting sects. To this day, the Church desires the authority to supply teachers and curriculum for teaching religion in all schools, with non-Catholics having the privilege of leaving a classroom during such sessions. In some countries, the Church desires complete administration of all public education. Juan Peron's rise to power in Argentina was abetted by the Church because he agreed to relinquish State power over education to the Church. His fall from power was aided by the Church because he made divorce a civil matter, and in other respects offended and decreased the power of the Church.

Antagonism to the Church was increased in the decades after independence in practically all the countries because the liberals advocated a secularization of national thought. The Church invariably sided with the conservatives. In the battle between centralism and federalism, the Church sided with the conservatives, who were anticentralist, because of their fear of what liberals and radicals could accomplish when they assumed power. In the nineteenth century, the constant fear of the Church was expropriation of its wealth and property. The oligarchies and social hierarchies, being committed to the retention of the status quo, always had the Church as an ally. This mutuality of purpose exists in most nations to this day and helps to feed the fires of anticlericalism.

The persistent fight of the Church for its rights, as it sees them, has led to an almost noncompromising position. When Ecuador signed a concordat with the Vatican in 1873, Presi-

dent García Moreno abandoned the *patronato real,* restored
the monopoly of education to the Church, empowered it to
censor all publications, and consecrated the republic to the
"Sacred Heart of Jesus." All these rights and privileges were
later lost when there was a turn of events. Today, the Church in
Ecuador has little influence, its properties have been nationalized, and its control over education removed. It receives a
pension from the State for its support.

In Venezuela, the government supplies substantial financial support for the Church, but the State exercises ecclesiastical patronage as successor to the *patronato real.* The status of
the Church in the various countries illustrates the lack of
consistency of Church-State relations in Latin America. One
is tempted to prognosticate that in some of the nations, the
current relationship is subject to change if the Church ceases
to be apolitical and if Protestantism becomes a real challenge
to the strength of Catholicism among the ranks of the masses.

John J. Johnson observes that "the Church and Catholic
lay organizations in league with the middle sector political
leadership might inject into politics a moral force for the most
part lacking at present" (29:192). If some of the ruling military
juntas in Chile, Peru and Brazil fall from power, it is predicted
there will be twelve or more Christian Democratic parties in
Latin America. They will be liberal and will have stemmed
from Catholic Action Committees. Their orientation will be
Catholic social justice falling somewhere between the philos-
ophies of Popes John XXIII and Paul VI.

Thus far, the Church generally has failed to be a potent
force for social justice. Its influence (mainly toward faith, but
increasingly toward social justice) is exerted on the mestizos,
who are the nucleus of the middle sector. The mestizos,
however, are also susceptible to demagoguery. They believe in
the centralization of power, since it is the politicians who
satisfy their material needs. States and towns in all the countries have become vassals of the federal powers. Thus,
although the mestizo goes to church, his behavior is guided by
the demands of the local *jefe politico.* Furthermore, in spite of
machismo, the Church is female-oriented. The Virgin repre-

sents the female *eros* (as per Plato, the emotional) and not the Christ, representing the male *logos* (the rational, doctrinal formalized by St. Thomas Aquinas).

The expansion of public education for those who constitute a middle sector, an economic middle class, has resulted in greater centralization of power since responsibility is concentrated in the central authorities. The central authorities ignore spiritual or moral values. They seek to develop a sense of nationalism. The Church is either blind or indifferent to this trend as long as it operates its own schools. These schools are, on the whole, superior to the public schools, but the existence of economic discrimination among them is evident. One can see at a glance which Catholic schools are for the scions of the wealthy and which are for those whose parents scrimp and deprive themselves of all luxuries in order to supply such things as a required school uniform. Latin American schools, public and private, require a school uniform for students.

There are other aspects, however, of the place of the Virgin or "Virgins" in Latin American Catholicism which require understanding. To non-Latins, the Virgin is Mary, the mother of Jesus, who was white and a Jewess. There are millions of Latin American Catholics who do not know of Mary's faith and color. Her relationship to Jesus, while known, is not of prime importance to them. As previously discussed, the Virgin has been catapulted into equal rank with the Father, the Son, and the Holy Ghost.

To complicate further the situation, there are several "Virgins" in Mexico who are equally venerated and who are not identified with Mary or Jesus. Those who worship a non-Guadalupiana Virgin have little awareness of the maternal relationship between the Madonna and the Child. These other Virgins are referred to by the noted anthropologist Eric Wolf (72:19).

After reading about the numerous "Virgins" who are venerated by lower-class Mexicans, an investigation was made to (a) verify the existence of this phenomenon, and (b) if true, discover the characteristics of the belief and the variances between the disciples or believers in the different female members of the Godhead. The color of the clothing was the first distinguishing feature to be mentioned by the great majority of those who spoke of the independent Virgins as separate entities without any relationship (much less identity) with each other. The Virgin of Guadalupe was unanimously considered to be the most colorfully dressed. The Virgin of Los Remedios wore the most somber clothing and she was a *chaparita*, shorty. All of them were equal in the performance of miracles. There appear to be six Virgins (religious) in Mexico. In Guadalajara, the Virgin of Popoan is a local semideity.

A considerable number of females who were interrogated identified each of the six virgins with Mary, but they did not know why these virgins had "geographical" or Church names instead of Maria. A minority knew of the relationship between Mary and Jesus. (Those interrogated were of the servant girl class, and only one out of twenty had more than a sixth grade education. Most had the equivalent of three years of schooling.) To most people, the statue of the Virgin is the personification of a deity, and to touch her statue after the purchase and lighting of a candle is assurance of succor. A monetary contribution, if possible, adds insurance to the expected fulfillment of one's requests.

In countries where Roman Catholicism is practiced, the paintings and other representations of the Virgin Mary usually show her with the infant Jesus. Almost without exception every famous work of art is titled "The Madonna and Child." In Latin America, practically every taxi, bus, and other means of public conveyance has a figure, or picture, of the Virgin dressed in silks and bedecked in jewels. The attire, finery, and resplendence is the representation of how she is depicted in the churches. She stands in all her pristine glory without any child in her arms. Jesus is hardly ever seen as a child. Some of the public conveyances carry pictures of the suffering Jesus.

Every taxi, and practically all buses, have an image of Jesus or Mary close to the driver. Some of the pictures, or statues, are enshrined with artificial flowers, lace curtains, and a small bulb, usually lit, over all. Taxi drivers in most countries have "their day" each year during which they attend a service outside of the cathedral or church to be blessed and also have their vehicles blessed. The animals also have their annual day on which to be blessed, and there are days for persons named Manuel, Concepción, and a few fortunate others.

The gap between religion and atheism is symbolized in several countries. Many new large businesses owned by Catholics have gala openings with a bishop in attendance to bless the endeavor. Smaller enterprises have the local priest present to offer a prayer for success. For the opening of establishments without devout Catholic interests, the Secretary of Commerce and Industry, or other ranking government officials, usually attend. Clergy or secular leaders are present to offer their blessing and to call upon the appropriate powers-to-be to spread good fortune upon the entrepreneurs.

An eternity of hell and damnation is beyond the mestizo's thinking. In the first place, the concepts of purgatory and hell were unknown to his Indian ancestors. Mayans, Aztecs, Quechuas, and Chibchas dwelt little on a life hereafter, but knowledge that there was a period of darkness after death. The spirit of the deceased remained in this stygian blackness for a limited period and then emerged again into light and a new life. This might be considered a form of reincarnation. The Latin American religious syntheses between Jesus and the Apostles and the Indians' gods and minor deities which occurred did not include such Christian concepts as hellfire and brimstone.

There was another type of syncretism which permitted monks and priests to believe that their converts were devout Catholics. The Indians from north to south used the names of Jesus and all his saints and uttered them with great devotion. These names, however, were to them aliases for the pantheon of gods adored by their ancestors. Quetzalcoatl, the high god of the Aztecs, became Jesus, and the lesser deities of the

Indians were given the names of the Apostles. The switch of names from Quetzalcoatl to Jesus was facilitated by two requirements that the Amerindians had imposed upon their chief deity: he had to lead a life of celibacy and had to refrain from inebrity.

Melville J. Herskovits in *The Myth of the Negro Past* refers to the concept of syncretism as used by the Brazilian anthropologist, Arthur Ramos (27:xxii). Ramos used the term in describing how the members of the African cults that have been preserved in Bahia are faithful Catholics who "identify their African deities with the saints of the Church." Herskovits reports that this same phenomenon has also been found in Catholic Cuba and Haiti and other parts of the New World.

Where a synthesis of Christianity and paganism was impossible because of an irreconcilability of beliefs, the acceptable aspects were taken from the former and the distasteful ones were discarded. William Madsen, author of *Christo-Paganism* (New Orleans, 1957), called his work a study of religious syncretism and ably depicted the process by which the end was achieved.

The mestizo is amoral. He learned centuries ago that professing Catholicism was as efficacious as practicing the faith. Since religious practice did not alleviate his burdens, did not make his place more secure, and did not improve his food, clothing, and shelter, whatever advantage accrued from being Catholic was achieved just as well by docile acceptance. An example of this dichotomy can be seen in the attitudes toward the sacrament of marriage. Mexican official statistics for 1961 show that at least 50 percent of the children in the country were born out of wedlock. The 1960 decennial census in Mexico shows that 90 percent of the people profess Catholicism. W. L. Schurz reported that the illegitimacy rate for births in Peru in 1943 was 45 percent, and that there were only 20,000 marriages in a population of seven million. In four provinces of Argentina, the rate of "natural" births (a beautiful euphemistic word to replace "illegitimate") for 1962 to 1966 was 43, 44, 46, and 66 percent (59:338). In a Costa

Rican survey, young single women placed marital fidelity in fifth place among traits desirable in their future husbands, while married women ranked it fourteenth.

Professor Wigberto Jiménez Moreno's admonition that anthropologists study Mexican ethnohistory before they attempt to describe modern Mexican culture applies to all of Latin America. Madsen in his *Christo-Paganism* avers that "folk Christianity often differs so strikingly from orthodox Christianity that it is misleading to call both types of religion by the same name" (41:111). At best, Latin American Catholicism can be called Spanish, rather than Roman. For the masses of people, Christo-Paganism is a better term. A partial explanation for the fatalism of the Mesoamerican Indian descendants is that their first gods created man and woman. This human couple were to give birth to *macehuales,* peasants, who would always be obliged to work and would find no pleasure in life.

The problems of the Church are creating schisms within the populace. While the conflict between the young, liberal priests and the older establishment cardinals and bishops receives publicity, there is a greater schism which, like an iceberg, is only partially above the surface. F. S. C. Northrup (Yale) stated that the main factor in the development of thought and culture during the past 120 years has not been the great issue between Spanish and Portuguese on the one hand and Indians and Africans on the other. He contends that the issue stems from the conflict between modern philosophical, political, economic, and clerical, and even antireligious ideas with Roman Catholic medievalism emanating from Europe (45:8). North America is Protestant and is influenced by the Reformation while Latin America is Catholic influenced by the Renaissance.

The "old" Catholicism is a totalitarian institution which conditioned the individual to authoritarianism rather than to democracy. If Latins were more prone to evolution, rather than revolution, the essence of pure religion (ethics and morálity) might have been preserved and democracy achieved.

6 ● The Family

The family is the primary social institution in all Latin American society. The concept of family is that of the extended family; parents, children, grandparents, aunts, uncles and cousins to the third and fourth degrees, rather than the nuclear family composed only of parents and children. The Latin American family is a closely-knit group including three or more generations and all in-laws, godparents, and cousins. Nepotism and family favoritism are legitimate obligations and supersede all other loyalties.

The respect for parents is very marked in the lower economic circles and among the rural, provincial peoples. Adult children will kiss the hand of their mothers and occasionally those of their fathers if they haven't seen each other for a week or more. Parents will not hesitate to sharply reprimand adult children in the presence of others and are unmindful of any accruing embarrassment, if any, to the adult child.

Another important characteristic of the family is the inclusion of *padrinos*, godparents, in the extended family unit. In the States, we have godmothers and godfathers whose designation is only honorary. In Latin America, godparents are vested with great responsibility for raising a child in the event he or she becomes an orphan. The godparents of a girl supply her trousseau and pay the costs of her wedding. Children and godparents always observe each other's birthdays, saint's days, and all other occasions that call for the presentation of gifts, and especially, respect to the elderly. Cuba is an exception in that godparents are primarily spirtual mentors and the material responsibilities are minimal.

The system of *compadrazgo** is especially important in the lower economic levels. It was practiced in Spain prior to the fifteenth century and is an adaptation of Spanish culture that is now Hispano-American. During the colonial period, we find several hundred cases in the various tribunals of the Holy Office of the Inquisition arising from the statement made by the *compadre,* the godfather, to the *comadre,* godmother, that sexual relationships between *compadrazgos* is not a sin. In these cases, the godfather was soliciting the godmother (not his wife) or the mother of his godchild. It is apparent that this relationship was viewed by the male as almost equivalent to a marital relationship. Many women solicited apparently didn't share the same attitude or concept, and reported these solicitations. The Inquisition executed heavy fines and imposed spiritual penance on the *compadre.*

The structure of the Latin American family is based on two premises:

(1) the supreme authority of the father while he chooses to retain the role of husband and father;

(2) the self-sacrificing mother ready to assume responsibility for the family in the face of desertion by her spouse.

---

*Defined by Edwin B. Williams as "compaternity." It is used to designate the relationship between a godfather and godmother or between a godfather and the parents of the child.

These premises originate from belief in the biological or natural superiority of the male over the female. This male prominence is also found in the preference for boys over girls in the family. The latter are welcomed in the family if they are born after the birth of two or three sons.

The role of the girls consists in taking care of her male siblings in order to allow her mother to devote herself to her husband. The girls begin early to help their mothers in household chores, and, in the lowest classes, to help with all the children except the one at the breast. The boys soon develop into their hypermasculine role, but all children pay the same strong respect to their parents. It appears that mothers pay more attention to their sons.

The machismo concept is implanted early in childhood and is impressed on both sexes. In the male, it includes sexual experience, but only with certain classes of women. Women are divided into two categories:

(1) one who symbolizes the mother image. She is chaste, religiously conforming, and sweet. These characteristics are regarded as admirable and desirable by the males in the lower middle and poor classes. In this group are the mother, sisters, and prospective brides.

(2) the second category encompasses all of the females in the world except those in the first group.

A pretty American girl in one of my classes in Mexico was taking her Junior year abroad. She once told me that while walking from the Hotel Maria Isabela to the Hotel Presidente—a few blocks distant and in the heart of the tourist area—she had received several proposals from young Mexicans. I asked her if she spelled proposals "propositions." She admitted that these were what the proposals turned to within minutes after a meeting. In the other countries where unaccompanied single American girls are few, similar proposals occur only in university circles. The cultured or well-to-do Latin male differentiates between women of his class and nationality, to whom he accords respect, and foreign women of the same group whose greater social freedom and patent desire for vicarious experiences seem to be an invitation to advances.

Dr. Rogelio Díaz Guerrero, in *Estudios de Psciologia del Mexicano* (11:11-24), has found that 44 percent of Mexican women over eighteen years of age are neurotic, while the percentage of males is over 32 percent. He attributes these high percentages to such conflicts as the clashing of traditional values with external reality. The role of sex is one of the areas of conflict. During the courtship period, the woman is idealized and exalted, but this state ends abruptly after the honeymoon. Roles are then reversed. The idealization process is now directed toward the husband, and the woman moves into an almost slavelike stage. Modern trends have contributed to marital discord since the old way has not been replaced completely by the new. Some question the validity of the old ways. Until recent times, the woman was mainly responsible for providing the entire family with religious orientation, love, tenderness, and sentimentality.

The modern Latin American woman is no longer content to be subjugated. She seeks equality, and most males have surrendered to a degree. Whether in Mexico, Costa Rica, Brazil, or Chile, one can see, on a Sunday or holiday, fathers carrying their children, romping with them and their wives in public parks, and enjoying being family men and sharing the responsibilities of parenthood with their wives. Families are diminishing in size, although a population explosion still exists among the poor and illiterate.

The male in his late teens has many male friends, and most of their social activities are totally masculine. It is not unusual to see groups of men of all ages dining together in restaurants on Saturday evenings and holidays. Girls and women are frequently excluded from their social world. The females, therefore, are compelled to seek companionship from the ranks of their own sex. It is not unusual on a Saturday night to see groups of two, three, or four attractive, well-dressed young girls from eighteen to twenty-five, unaccompanied by any males, at the cinema. Similarly, one can see groups of young men at the same places, but there are few attempts at "pick-ups."

The change in roles now in progress has been produced by the presence of women in business, in the university as students as well as teachers, in the increase in literacy, the access to television in the urban areas and radios in the smallest hamlet or *pueblito,* and in the awakening of thoughts of equality in women. Only in the pure Indian areas are women still living (living fairly contentedly, we should add) as did their ancestors of centuries ago.

This change may be illustrated by a conversation I had several years ago in Mexico City with an attractive and brilliant young Mexican woman who had earned two advanced degrees, and was multilingual. She asked me if I knew any single Jewish men of her age (about twenty-five or older) because she wanted to meet some. Since we were friends, I asked her the reason. She said that she had matrimonial intentions. When I expressed surprise at her interest in a Jew as a prospective spouse, she said, "I am running out of dates with my fellow Catholic countrymen. When I have a date, I must listen to all their statements and opinions, some foolish or even infantile, and nod my head in agreement. If I succeed in keeping my mouth closed, I am asked for a second date. The second time, I sometimes venture to express my opinion or disagree with my escort. If I am not too vehement, there might be a third date, but this usually is the last because by then I fail to restrain myself and act and speak as his equal."

She then continued, "I want a Jewish husband for other reasons than his permitting me to speak as his peer. Jewish men are noted for greater stability. As the wife of a Jew, I will be able to count on his being home for dinner every night. I will be accorded respect. I'll know or at least have an idea of where he is and the children will be ours—not mine alone. I'll not be waiting nights wondering whether he is at a casa chica."

Two years later, and without my aid, the young woman

married a Jew. They are happily married and have three children. The number of professing, but not practicing, Catholic young women who are converting to Judaism in order to marry Jewish spouses is considerable in Mexico, Brazil, and Argentina. Not all formally convert to Judaism, but their children are often reared in the Jewish faith. On the other hand, there are many Jewish youths who are abandoning the faith of their ancestors. They are drifting away and assimilating into the great group of agnostics to be found in the higher economic circles.

The welfare of children is set forth in several governmental constitutions. In Panama and Uruguay there is a provision that parents are obliged to support and educate children, who, in turn, are to respect and assist their parents. There is a reciprocal obligation. Children are entitled to equal treatment regardless of legitimacy of birth. In some countries, the marital status of parents may be omitted. In some countries, birth records do not reveal any data pertaining to the father. The Bolivian Constitution provides that "marriage, the family and maternity are under the protection of the State."

The status of a wife may result from a "free union" (analogous to the American common law status) or from a legal ceremony. There is no stigma to "free unions," and the female has all the rights of inheritance and support of a legal spouse, provided that there is no legal spouse.

Life to the mestizo means survival through struggle, and survival can be achieved only by the exercise of his own wits and toil. The struggle recurs each day. The pleasures and comforts of eternity, the vision of what awaits him in some heavenly paradise in the life hereafter are too abstract for many. The mestizo *campesino* has little sense of time or space. He knows only the day and the limits of his field and pueblito. While most Western people work to live, the mestizo lives to work.

His work and contacts during work supply the topics of conversation in his home. The same applies to the urban street vendor. The story is told of María, who arose early each morning to go to the wholesale fruit and produce market to buy fifty oranges. She would then wend her way to the district where she sold her wares. One day, one of her regular customers who bought two or three oranges each day after polite haggling over the price, offered to buy her entire stock because of an approaching family fiesta. Maria refused to sell her entire supply even though the customer stated that he was willing to buy without bargaining. Maria finally explained her persistent refusal by telling him that if he bought all her wares the first thing in the morning, she would have nothing to do the balance of the day, and she would have nothing to recount to her family.

Maria's social life consisted of her encounters with various people and her narration of the day's events. The customer who knows how to parry words and bandy them with the small vendor will always get a lower price, because the vendor's repertoire of the stories of the day's sales will be enlarged and the lower price is a reward for supplying repeatable conversation.

The wife is not concerned with what she will feed her family on the morrow. Each day presents sufficient problems. Menu planning is left to the affluent and sophisticated. She is content if she awakens in the morning and knows that she has the *massa,* dough, from which to make her tortillas, or, for the city dwellers, the centavos to pay for a kilo (2.2 pounds) or two of tortillas, and that she has the beans, rice, and two or three eggs, or some chicken feet or a piece of meat and a bone.

In the city, there is also a market, but here, in contrast to the rural market, one does not see the Indians of the woods or the *campesino* or the bedraggled native of doubtful parentage and unknown origin. Customers run the gamut of all economic classes. Spread on the ground or on carts or in stalls are wares of all kinds: antiques, both legitimate and fraudulent; objects that are gaudy and tinsel-like to catch the eye; instruments and tools of all trades and professions; and old rusty nails and other things beyond any functional state.

Each pile will attract a buyer—even the pile of nails so rusty that they will bend at the slightest blow.

To what use will they put those rusted hinges or rusty nails? They may never be put to use at all, but they will symbolize property and will make the purchaser an owner and possessor of a material object. It is difficult to comprehend the emptiness in the life of a person who craves to own some rusty nails so that he or she can say, "This is mine." According to our standards, the purchase is madness, but it must be compared to our purchase of a hat that we do not need or a gadget that we will never use. The affluent society finds it outlandish of these people to squander hard-earned funds so foolishly. We had Latin American maids who took from my wastepaper basket discarded empty cartridges from my ballpoint pen. They were completely useless, but they represented treasures to the maids. My wife and I became local heros in a rural one-room school in Guatemala because we distributed ten ballpoint pens that we had received gratis in the States as an advertising souvenir.

The first reason that maids, *muchachas*, submit to sexual relationships is vanity; they believe that they are attractive to someone, that some male wants them because "she is she." They do not know or realize that the male would have resorted to any other woman to satisfy his momentarily overcharged libido. Their second reason for submission is that they want to conceive. The child will be theirs. The child will be a possession. They want a child, even one born out of wedlock, despite their attendance at mass on Sundays and holy days and at communion. They rarely go to confession. They know that there is little or no stigma attached to them or to the child born illegitimately.

The mestiza knows that the child born from her womb will be hers, and hers alone. She will not share the child with its father unless she so chooses. She does not ask for support for the child from the father. She also knows that the child will not serve as a hindrance to finding employment as a house servant. Servants have separate quarters, and employers have learned that a maid with a child prefers to remain with one family rather than change posts once a year as many do. Those who make changes do so for fear that they might become emotionally attached to the employer's family and such attachment might reduce loyalty to their own families or hinder opportunities for marriage. When a maid feels that she is a part of the family, even as a menial, she sometimes relinquishes her few hours of freedom on Sunday, thereby losing the opportunity of meeting males at the home of friends or relatives. Orphanages and babies for sale are rarer in Latin America than they are in the United States.

Pilferage by maids is an accepted part of employer-employee relationships. The mistress of the house frequently carries a chain with keys for every drawer, every cupboard, every closet in the house, and sometimes even for the refrigerator. She counts the dirty linen and then counts the laundry (always done at home, and often in cold water) after washing and ironing. In spite of all her efforts, a handkerchief will sometimes be missing, a bar of soap disappear, or some pins, rarely anything of real value. When the mistress discovers a loss, she makes no accusation unless she wants to discharge the maid. However, she will comment so that the maid knows that the mistress is not being hoodwinked. The maid who is a thief usually absconds with something of value. The pilferers merely desire something small and insignificant. They feel no remorse for taking, and do not regard themselves as thieves or as sinners. The bar of soap might have been taken to give to a mother. If and when amoral people are caught, they feel regret at being apprehended, but no remorse for the act of which they are accused.

Most Americans mistake Latin American courtesy for cordiality and friendship. We are charmed when a Latin American says, *"con permiso,"* "with your permission," when he leaves. Some Americans are sufficiently naive to believe in the sincerity of the oft-repeated phrases such as *"Mi casa es su casa,"* "my house is your house"; or, when an address is requested, the Latin will add to his address *"a su casa,"* "at your house." Of course, few Americans realize that they have not seen the inside of the home or apartment of the Latin American with whom they had been negotiating a commercial affair, or to whom they had brought some message. A wealthy Latin will have taken him to a public restaurant or to his club for lunch or dinner, but not to his domicile. The poor and middle class choose not to display their humble abodes.

The home and family of Latin Americans are reserved for the general family and intimate friends. The Latin regards his family and his family life as personal and private. He is averse to having them subjected to intrusions by those not within the inner circle of family intimates. The cosmopolite, the world traveler, is an exception since he knows the tastes and desires of American friends.

The acceptance of plural female relationships is reflected in some of the penal systems, some aspects of which we are learning to imitate in America. Many Latin American penal systems have visiting days for wives and separate ones for mistresses. The days for mistresses are never on Sunday, since they are family visiting days. There are private rooms in the jails where each prisoner may meet his wife and enjoy conjugal pleasures without the peering eyes of prison guards. On other days, he may meet with his paramour. Prostitutes are available for those who have no female companion on the outside who would share a cot with the prisoner for the allotted time.

While there is hardly any condemnation of "free unions" and women bearing children without being legally married (even having four children each sired by another male), there is condemnation of public nudity and semi-nudity on the cover of magazines. The disapproval of a maximum exposure of the female body does not extend to the beaches of Acapulco, Copocabana in Rio de Janeiro, or the beaches outside of Buenos Aires. The personal beliefs of the ruler of the country often play a great role in the laxity or enforcing of laws against pornography. For several years one could buy *Playboy* and a few Latin American magazines that did not go as far as Hefner's monthly magazines. However, most ruling military groups, possibly to appease and win support of the Church, ban magazines with pictures of nudes of either sex. Mrs. Maria Esther Zuno de Echeverria, the wife of the Mexican president, and the mother of their eight children and a devout Catholic, not only had marriages performed in a cinema house for over 1,000 Mexican couples who were living "in sin" but she also began a campaign in 1972 against pornography. She said, "We must unite to form an authentic public conscience. Publications which put themselves at the margin of the law for their immorality must be rejected from the bosom of society." The Mexican newspaper, *El Sol,* the voice of the conservatives and the Church, at the end of April 1972 called for a governmental war against pornography.

7 ● The Middle Class

There are substantial differences between the middle class in highly industrialized Western nations and Latin America. Peter Nehemkis discusses the differences in his book, *Latin America: Myth and Reality* (44:passism). Schurz holds that the middle class in Latin America is composed of the mestizos and is not comparable in any aspect to the position of the middle class in the United States (59:308).

John Gerassi divides literate Latin Americans into "medievalists" and "modernists" (18A:14-15). The former are dedicated to the maintenance of the status quo whether it be religious, social, or economic. He states that for medievalists "liberty is more important than health, and freedom a richer food than bread." The modernist espouses "dignity" and opposes exploitation. The modernist knows that freedom is the result, not the cause, of well-being. What appears to be an anachronism to the American is that the medievalist is for freedom of the press while the modernist would give the tools to people to build a true freedom, but would not allow them a free press during the process of building. President Allende of Chile illustrated this as does President Velasco of

Peru and the military junta, now led by General Pinochet, which overthrew Allende. The middle class or middle sector is represented by the above medievalists.

There are many knowledgeable Hispano-Americanists who have dared to say that the Latin American masses are not ready for democracy and that during the process of learning the meaning and appreciating the fruits of democracy, the people must be governed by a benevolent dictatorship of one man or a small group. Although it is impossible to refute the correctness of this argument, the lessons of history must not be forgotten. Latin America has had a few benevolent dictators, but they either forgot or overlooked the ultimate goal: democracy for their people. They were so preoccupied with economic problems and their aides so busy lining their own pockets that true freedom for the masses was relegated to the coming of some other messiah.

The middle class of our neighbors to the south is composed of people who are essentially conformists or traditionalists. They desire to advance themselves materially (as do their counterparts in America) so that they may share in the benefits of those who are in the class above them. They want to exploit their laborers and employees, and they want to be on the receiving end of the fruits of corruption and chicanery. A wealthy individual once commented on the manipulation of government contracts and political influence. I asked him how he felt about this, and whether he did not want things to change. His reply was, "Why should I want any changes? I would like to be there myself and I would show those whom I displace what can be really made." Others interviewed in several countries made similar responses. There were differences in the wording, but the sentiments were the same.

The distinguished Chilean scholar and economist, Claudio Velez, wrote about the middle class, or sector, in *The World Today:*

> The fundamental error in the U.S. approach has to do with
> the definition of the middle class. U.S. scholars, politicians and

journalists have gleefully discovered a Latin American middle class and without pausing to find out what kind of middle class it really is, they have proceeded to credit it with all sorts of qualities it does not possess. In fact, the only claim which the Latin American urban middle class has to the description "middle class" is based on the fact that they are in the middle, between the traditional aristocracy and the peasants and the workers.

Frederick B. Pike in *Chile and the United States* comments:

> Chile's urban middle sectors have traditionally demonstrated colossal indifference to the social problems and have dedicated themselves to defending the value judgments of the upper class. . .the readily observable traits of the middle class have led to the introduction into the Chilean vocabulary of the word *siútico*. A siútico is a middle class individual who emulates the aristocracy and its adages and hopes to be taken for one of its members. [See also Frederick G. Gil, *The Political System of Chile*. Boston, 1966, p. 27] [50:284-285].

Pike also stated that one of the results of the 300-year Spanish rule was that the colonials "ostentatiously pro-claimed their lack of association with manual productive labor or any kind of vile employment" (51:78). The fostering of the get-rich-quick mentality of the conquistadors also left its imprint on the Latin American psyche. The continuation of many preindustrial values may readily stem from the persistence of the rural social structures which contributed to the creation of the foregoing values.

The authoritarianism of the Catholic Church in spiritual matters may well have been translated into authoritarianism by lay leaders in other facets of the life of the people. But any value system derived from given sets of historical experience institutionalized in religious systems, family structures, class relations, and education will affect the pace and even direction of social and economic change (19B:75).

Aaron Lipman differentiated some large-scale Latin American entrepreneurs from the above comments when he wrote, "They are urban people in a rural country [Colombia] in a relatively traditionally oriented society but their values are rational and modern" (34B:30). On the other hand, there is Argentina which stands very high among the most developed Latin American nations because of its high literacy and urbanization but whose citizens have little loyalty to universalist aspects of the state. Despite Peron's debacle as a ruler and national leader and his death on July 1, 1974, Peronismo still exists in 1975 and the majority feel loyalty to him and now to his widow rather than to the state. "Peronismo" means whatever the "right" or "left" wants. It is a term without definite meaning.

The Mexican bourgeoisie is different from that of other Ibero-American countries. Mexican bourgeoisie consists of well-to-do mestizos who haven't succeeded in completely sloughing off characteristics of their original role in Mexican society. But they, as do many other similar Latin Americans in the operations of their businesses, prefer low volume and a high mark-up. The role of the Mexican bourgeoisie has been held far too long and its implanted effect cannot be dropped in a generation.

In other Hispano-American nations, the bourgeoisie is the oligarchy. They are the *hacendados,* the large farmers, the ranchers, and the plantation owners. They oppose change in their four-century-old status quo. One can read in Peruvian papers to this day of lands being offered for sale "with 300, more or less, Indians."

Unlike the middle class of the United States of America, the Latin American middle sector is devoid of any sense of community responsibility or moral obligation to the impoverished. (Only the poor share with each other.) The middle class or sector does dispense some charity. Sometimes there is pressure from a local political chief but whatever is done is done on an individual basis. The middle sector does not agitate since they live behind walls and are mentally and socially isolated from their fellowman.

William L. Schurz terms the Latin American middle class "an interim group," and he considers it to be growing in numbers and influence in Argentina, Chile, Uruguay, and southern Brazil. (Coincidentally, the four countries that he cites are heavily populated by Germans, who began coming in the late 1840s, and by Jews, whose large-scale immigration began after World War I except in Argentina, where they established many agricultural settlements beginning in 1890, and by Italians who have been coming since the 1880s.)

It is generally understood that the middle group is composed of professional men, upper echelon government white-collar workers, merchants—excluding small shop-keepers—executives of large businesses, and independent large-scale farmers. An important characteristic of this group is that they are of a cultural level above the average and are endowed with certain social graces. It is they and the Communists who have turned nationalism into a political doctrine and who vent their spleen against the United States (33:223).

John J. Johnson refuses to use the term "middle class" (29:vii, 3). He states that the "middle sectors" of Latin America only recently had an economic connotation. These people are grouped by learning, prejudice, conduct, way of life, background, and aesthetic sentiments. They do not necessarily share a common background of experience, which Johnson considers the central condition of a class.

The members of the middle groups, or sectors, are interested in personal aggrandizement and advancement, and "their minds are ruled more by their immediate material needs than by reason" (29:182). They are centralists in government conduct and adhere to *personalismo* or *caciquismo* in politics because it facilitates making arrangements with government bureaus and officialdom. Jacques Lambert also prefers "middle sector" to middle class (33:81) and he confines its political influences to the A. B. C. countries (Argentina, Brazil and Chile), Mexico, Uruguay, and Venezuela. They are a potent force only in the large cities. Gerassi credits Mexico with the largest number, "but not so big as some historians would have us believe" (18:124).

The maintenance of *personalismo* helps to keep workers in subordinate positions. The president, or local *jefe politico*, becomes the Great White Father. He is the *patrón* and stands as *pater familias*, which places him above and beyond approach. In societies as materialistic as those of Latin America (despite protestations that they are not materialistic), social gains are subordinated to material gains. The *patrón* who has received some unusual windfall will dispose largesse with an open hand to those dependent on him or his constituency.

Licenciado Miguel Alemán served as president of Mexico from 1946 to 1952. During his term of office, some Mexicans, sotto voce, called him *el bandito*. They then added that, despite this title, for every two dollars that came into his hands, one dollar always trickled through his fingers to the general populace. For this reason, signs were surreptitiously posted in Mexico City during 1961-1962 calling for the return of *"el bandito"* because the then President Adolfo López Mateos had fallen into disfavor.

The middle and upper groups send their children to parochial and private schools. This tends to perpetuate social distinctions. However, the increasing number of children who attend the public schools and the growth of the urban populations are awakening a desire for a better life among the working class. This demand is being met in part by social welfare benefits, such as medical care for workers and their families, and a government pension system for the elderly. Early in 1971, President Echeverria of Mexico arranged for government workers to buy Fiats or Renaults at reduced prices and at 10 percent finance charges.

One basic right is being denied the workers in most countries—the right to have an independent union. There are unions in most countries, but they are manipulated by *caudillos*. (A *caudillo* is a leader; e.g. General Franco's title is El Caudillo—it also implies a dictator.) Political activities are the main program of action. In several countries, Argentina and Mexico being two examples, a government bureau must first declare a strike to be legal. In the event it is held to be illegal, a not uncommon event, and workers proceed to strike, the government appoints an "intervenor" who assumes full control of the union and its treasury. The former union and strike leaders are jailed if they persist in flaunting the orders of the Labor Court.

The *Miami Herald* of October 18, 1969, carried an interesting article by Peter Laine. He reported that Latin labor leaders accused the hemisphere militarists of stifling trade union views and aspirations. The report of three labor leaders was made to the Organization of American States Assembly of Labor Ministers. Alfredo de Oacce, head of the Latin American Trade Union Confederation, accused Argentina, Brazil and Paraguay of suppressing trade union resolutions calling for freedom. He said, "We found a huge gap between the reports from the governments and the social and economic reality of the countries to which they belong."

If a strike is declared legal, however, all entrances to the premises are barred. A red and black flag or band is posted across all entrances. The union pitches tents at the street entrance and a twenty-four hour vigil is maintained by union members for the duration of the strike. Portable toilet facilities of the type placed on construction sites are next to the tents.

Bargaining is a way of life except in the large stores in the principal cities. It is a battle of wits. It is indulged in by people from all walks of life. The señora may, at times, relegate the duty to her maid or *muchacha*. Men are infrequent participants. Even the small *puestero* (owner of a stall in a market) delights in the matching of wits, and the dialogue of a successful sale is repeated almost verbatim to family and friends at night. One sees signs, *precio fijo*, "fixed price" or "one price," in stores on Corrientes or Florida, important shopping streets in Buenos Aires, or Avenida Madero in Mexico City. The absence of the sign except in obviously exclusive shops or department stores is an invitation to bargain.

Caveat emptor, "let the buyer beware," runs all through

Latin American negotiations. There is no impulse or urge to warn customers of limitations of use, of inherent dangers, or of latent defects. Latin American countries are years away from even thinking of consumer legislative protection. The price received by the seller is the highest that he can obtain from a purchaser. This is a well-understood game. Quality may enter into the discussion or haggling over the price, but discussion of quality is the means to arrive at the end, which is the price. After it is over, the seller may surreptitiously substitute something slightly damaged. An artisan may leave some inner part unfinished. There are a million and one petty ways of shortchanging or getting an additional picayune edge.

Yet, Latin America is creating a new culture. Culture is not used herein as a term for the arts, for the aesthetic facets of life. Culture, anthropologically defined, is a society's complete and total way of life from the womb to the tomb. The mestizo culture is amorphous and its value system has not yet been completely established. American, English, French, and German tourists and businessmen have made inroads on the Hispanic-American way of life, which is still evolving. The Hispanic-American cultures, having no inherent defense mechanism, have not developed the ability to resist. The likelihood is that mestizo culture will be some bastard version of what is known as Western civilization. The urban mestizo has a great apperceptive capacity. Because he is subject to the virus of envy and has a thirst for the position and things that his economic superiors enjoy, he is becoming aggressive and is assuming a superficial polish together with the new clothing he dons. Beneath the clothing and veneer of suavity and hypocritical courtesy, however, his individualism and egocentrism remain. He can be merciless and cruel, and, once aroused, cannot be easily placated.

The influences of Western culture insidiously and subtly are making advances in the urban areas. Advertising on billboards and roadsides, in magazines, newspapers, comic books, and soap operas on radio and TV are making all women sisters, not under the skin, but outside it.

United States salesmanship and the aspiration to imitate and attain the material affluence and style of life of our country have been accompanied by (or caused by) advertising, which uses American girls. This sets the model for all Latin American women except the Indian and the impoverished. This is somewhat akin to what happened in the United States prior to the advent of the Negro's search for self-pride. For instance, advertisements placed in the magazine *Ebony* by white advertisers showed white models until protest brought a replacement.

The substitution or imitation of American values has caused a chauvinistic reaction. A campaign has been started to restrict American magazines and even Spanish editions of *Reader's Digest* and *Good Housekeeping*, despite the fact that they are translated into Spanish and are printed in Latin America. There is also a movement in Mexico which will undoubtedly spread in a modified form to other areas of Central America if it persists beyond initial enthusiasm. It is known as "The Confederate Movement to Restore Anauak."

The Nahuatl name for the Valley of Mexico prior to the Spanish conquest was Anahuac (the use of the "c" rather than the "k" was the hispanized spelling). Nahuatl was the language spoken by the Aztecs in an area roughly between Puebla and Tlaxcala on the east, and the edge of the Tarrascan territory on the west, which began near the present city of Taxco.

This new confederation headed by Attorney Rodolfo Nieva does not seek a return to "the human sacrifices and feathered headgear of the Aztecs," but does seek to restore the "Mexican civilization." Nieva asserts that Mexican civilization was more advanced than the current (Western) one. There is mention of the restoration of Huitzilopochtli, one of the primary Aztec gods—the god of war and darkness. It is urged that Mexico be spelled "Meshiko" and that the Aztec calendar be utilized. Salazar Mallen, a syndicated columnist for the newspaper, *Novedades*, reported that the "movement's roots are not planted in love for Mexico or in its past, but in a hatred of everything Spanish."

For most people, while Indian names for some places have been restored and some Indian names are being used by people, pride in European, or "white," ancestry is most prevalent. It is evidenced in the preference of life styles, food, and social customs and values.

America must learn how to gain the goodwill and trust of the "middle sector." The revolutionary forces in Latin America stem from two of the groups within the middle sector: the military officer corps and the university students. These two groups are educated or trained for political activity and are organized for revolutionary action. These two groups have been educated in their countries' schools. Most have not progressed beyond the *secondaria*, high school, of the public school system. It is in these schools that there are subtle teachings which slant history against the United States. This exists even in the schools of those countries that are not critical of the United States and who maintain cordial relations. One thing that unites all Latin American countries, however, is the distrust of the "Colossus of the North."

We must learn that if we are to do business in Latin America, we must conduct ourselves within the context of their customs. American ways may be more efficient, but efficiency is an obstacle to understanding and approval. Most American-owned enterprises in Latin America tend to pay higher wages than their native competitors. One would think that the inducement of higher rate of pay would cause the local employees to choose to work for the American firms.

There are many who prefer to work for a local business at a lower wage. It is not chauvinism or loyalty to native firms which impel them to do so. The following is the explanation offered by some of the employees. They concede that a certain American firm pays higher wages, but "I must punch a clock when I enter and when I leave. If I am late, they make a deduction from my pay. If I leave early because my compadre has a fiesta on his saint's day, I am docked. If I do not come on Monday [sarcastically called San Lunes, Saint Monday, by employers; there is no such saint on the holy calendar, but it is the time to sleep off effects of the overindulgence on Sunday] or come in late, I lose some pay. My countryman does not make any such deductions."

Of course, the employee forgets that his countryman-employer makes him work beyond the regular quitting time when he comes late and that he is compelled to do other things to make up for time lost. The point here for American managers is that they have to adjust to the local customs. The employee feels a sense of independence in coming when he feels that he wants to come and that he is not penalized for his independence. This is a sense of liberty and equality which must be comprehended; to be deprived of that feeling is not compensated for by higher wages. In this instance, it is the American who has the short-sighted view of the value of materialism. Also involved is an important cultural difference in the manner of perceiving time.

There is another side to the coin of understanding the Latin American worker. We must also understand the Latin American industrialist. Most Latin American governments of today are controlled by small elites of military or the oligarchy—better yet, one of the oligarchies, since there are usually a few in each country, and the Church is usually one of them. The authors of *Elites in Latin America* contend that an understanding of the elites is necessary in order to understand the political, social, and economic processes in their countries (35:viii). One of the authors of this book discusses the new urban groups as one of the elites (35:61-93).

Luis Ratinoff, a Chilean sociologist, attributes the new forms of social inequality to the rapid urbanization in Hispanic America. Among the results of the rise to power of the middle sector is that it did not displace the traditional elite. There was a sharing of power between the old and new elite. In other respects, the middle sector remains amorphous as a power or elite because of the contradictory features and the absence of a definite trend. Ratinoff observes that "it has been repeatedly asserted that the middle class. . .lacked a real sense of direction" (35:75).

The outstanding characteristic of the merchants and industrialists of the middle sector (not necessarily mestizo), which is almost uniform in all of Latin America, is that they espouse a kind of economic nationalism predicated on industrialization manipulated by the state for their benefit.

Among some of the conclusions to be drawn as a result of the rise of the middle sector are: their power is to be for their own benefit, which is evidenced by the fact that the control of the social security systems is in the hands of the representatives of the middle sector; and "in many of the cases most of the benefit [of the social security systems] went to the dependent sectors of the middle class themselves" (35:86). It has also been noted that the benefits of labor legislation are little more than a verbalization of good intentions (35:87) and expansion of education is usually limited to urban areas (35:88), and that there are many contradictory features in Latin American middle classes.

The renowned sociologist of Harvard University Seymour Martin Lipset indicates that managerial appointments are made "on the basis of family links, rather than on a specialized training," and that "the maintenance of family prestige is a principal concern of the typical entrepreneur" (35:13).

Tomás Roberto Fillol, in *Social Factors in Economic Development* (14:13, 14), is the authority for the statement that in business, "outsiders are distrusted for the entrepreneur is acutely aware that any advantage that may be given to somebody outside his family is necessarily at the expense of himself and his own family. The types of managers employed by family groups are called *hombres de confianza*, men capable of being trusted."

Latin American nations are constantly striving for greater industrialization. The move of the rural population to urban centers aggravates the need to create more jobs, which are available only with increased industrialization. However, Latin businessmen labor under the delusion that the United States is a colossus because of our gadgets, autos, TV sets, radios, electronic and computer machines. They look at the result—the end product—and fail to see the system that has produced these machines and gimmickry. They ignore our democratic traditions, the personal freedoms, and the higher standards of living which were the fruits of our heritage and principles. They do not yet comprehend that the material aspects of one's culture are secondary to the basic premises upon which this culture rests—the glorification and edification of the individual.

Since any increase in the numbers of the middle class or middle sector must come from the mestizos or indigenous populace, Americans must become aware of the religious concepts and the value systems and recognize wherein they differ from ours. Amorality is the rule rather than the exception among the lower economic classes throughout Latin America. The Church has been unable to effect any change. In order to bring the illiterates and the rural populations into the twentieth century, we must accept the existence of a problem and, after acceptance, ascertain the means of inculcating standards of Christian morality and some changes in the value systems.

Professor Frank Lorimec of the American University, Washington, D.C., wrote, "The situation in Latin America which contains one-third of all adherents to the Catholic faith, is particularly acute. Among seventeen countries from which statistics are available, there are nine in which more than half of all births are illegitimate." In the absence of moral influence by the Church, then foreign investors must look for other forces to secure some moral standards among their staffs. The native entrepreneur plays the double role of macho and *patrón* to his employees.

While women are being liberated and being enfranchised, it is still felt that they should not be placed in posts where they are in a superior capacity to men. The enfranchised women have proven to be more conservative than men. The women in Chile defeated Salvador Allende in 1958. The Christian Democratic Party pandered to women by creating home-oriented skills for them. By 1970, Allende had learned how to manipulate women and he thereby had many of them defect from the Christian Democrats. Of course, he was aided by the spiralling inflation that his predecessors had failed to curb, much less control. Allende gave women posts in his party and had them play a larger role than their counterparts in the opposition parties. Unfortunately for him, he was overthrown by the Army and the Church, which are exclusive male organizations. Just as the Army was not unanimous in the view that Allende had to be removed from office, there were several in the Church hierarchy who deplored the attempted removal and his suicide.

Lipset wrote that in Latin American underdeveloped countries, there is a preservation of values which deters the systematic accumulation of capital. He stressed two factors in Latin American backgrounds which create a social structure "more congruent with ascriptive values." These are Catholicism and centuries-long domination by ruling elites (36:65).

Until such time as there is a greater emphasis in Latin America on achievement and a deference of respect for others on the basis of merit, economic progress must be slow. The foregoing applies to the industrial field as well as to the educational systems. Status as a party member or role-assignment due to family relationships preserves a self-defeating status quo. Lipset quotes Aldo E. Solar's *Estudios sobre la sociedad Uruguan:* "the middle class concerns are for security, moderation, lack of risk, and prestige" (36:69).

8 ● Anti-Hispanism—
The Indian

The dislike of most things Hispanic by many Latin Americans is hardly of recent origin. This rejection has manifested itself in many respects. Fernando Benítez in *The Century After Cortés* wrote that "the weakness of the Mexican and his serious limitations as compared with the Spaniard are attributable to the fact that he was born in a colony, an essential circumstance which we must always bear in mind in . . . the consideration of the Mexican character." Benítez continued a few pages later, "The colony is closer to us than we think. The 'deep sense of worthlessness,' the Mexican's famous inferiority complex . . . is an offshoot of the colony" (3:278-282).

Although Mexico gained its independence in 1821 and was recognized internationally as a nation, Spain did not accord it recognition until 1834. In 1827, Mexico expelled all Spaniards from its land. It is reputed that some 72,000 Spaniards had to leave. Spain later joined with England and France in 1862 in an abortive attempt to overrun Mexico in order to collect debts due them. England and Spain withdrew, and

France continued alone to establish the Empire under Maximilian and Carlotta.

During the 300-year period of Spanish domination of the New World criollos, mestizos and Indians, the mother country regarded its colonies as existing solely for exploitation and its inhabitants as little better than serfs. Spain's mercantile theory meant the taking of raw materials at the lowest possible cost from the natives and selling back to them the finished or manufactured products at the highest possible price with the imposition of a series of sales taxes called the *alcabola*, a tax on every transaction from the time of arrival at the ports of Veracruz and Acapulco in New Spain or Puerto Bello or Cartagena.

The Holy Office of the Inquisition was denied jurisdiction over the Indians because they were not regarded as *gente de razón*, people of reason. Indians were denied admission to most monastic orders and to the priesthood. We have previously indicated the Spaniard's concept of the mestizos and the disabilities of the criollos because of their birth in the New World. These disabilities existed despite the status of parents who were *peninsulares*, born in Spain. The officials of the *audiencias* and other Crown appointees were barred from marriage with any of the native born while they served in the New World.

The wars for independence waged in the first two decades of the nineteenth century were led by criollos or mestizos. The colonists revolted against Spain but never unified their efforts except in most of South America. Men such as Simon Bolivar, Vicente Guerrero, and Bernardo O'Higgins were products of the New World. One of the interesting characteristics of the revolts for independence was that they came at a time when the mestizos had attained a measure of economic success and the local populace had never had it so good since the time of the conquests.

Except for the Araucanians of Chile, the Indians had abandoned thoughts of regaining independence or a status of equality with Spaniards or mestizos. Resentment existed but no major attempt was made to alter the situation. Today, there are millions of Indians who are Catholic in name only and their mores are those of their ancestors. In parts of South America, especially in the Brazilian hinterlands and the east slopes of the Andes, Indians are still living in the Stone Age and most governments do little for them and care less about their fate or survival.

Hatred of the gachupin or peninsular Spaniard has not completely dissipated. Father Hidalgo gave the *grita de Dolores*, the shout of battle cry of Dolores (the town where he had his parish), that began the Mexican War for Independence on September 15, 1810. (Many Americans call Mexico's War for Independence a revolution because Americans call their war of 1776 the Revolutionary War. Mexicans call their internecine civil war of 1910-1917 "the Revolution.") Padre Hidalgo's shout was "Long live our Lady of Guadelupe! Death to the gachupin, and Ferdinand VII restored to the throne!" The war became one for independence several months later when the attempt to dethrone Joseph Bonaparte in Spain was thwarted. The first year of the War for Independence was a battle between the Brown Virgin, Our Lady of Guadelupe, who was claimed by the Indians and mestizos, and the White Virgin, the Holy Mother, whose banner was carried by the Spanish royalists. The gachupines, their sympathizers, and the royalists did not care who sat on the throne of Spain.

Adherents of the theory of homogeneity of Latin American nations stress the fact that they had been colonized and ruled by Spain for 300 years, which, they urge, created a common culture and language. If anything is shared in common, it is a hatred of Spain by many of the nations because of the cruelty of the Spanish administration. We should not confuse Spain and Spaniards. Most Hispano-Americans now like the Spaniards. Their dislike is of the government and the kings of the past and the nature of the present Spanish regime. All Latin American nations have recognized Franco as El Caudillo and maintain diplomatic relations with Spain—except Mexico. While there are trade missions between the nations, diplomatically Spain does not exist for Estados Unidos de Mexico. One of the differences between the founding of the thirteen colonies and the colonies founded by Spain lay in the basic policy—the North American colonies were founded "so that people might live, while the Spanish colonized so that people could loot."

Leopold Zea quotes from Victorino Lastarria as follows:

> The Spaniards conquered America, soaking its soil in blood, not to colonize it, but rather to take possession of the precious metals that it produced so abundantly. [Zea then added that when Spain attempted to colonize] Spain transplanted . . . all the vices of her absurd system of government, and to these vices were added the scorn that the peninsular [Spaniard] felt for . . . the mestizo. The mestizo became the bastard of America. [76:57]

The Chilean, Francisco Bilbao, in his *Sociabilidad Chilena,* declared that "our past is the Spain of the Middle Ages" whose body and soul "was Catholicism and feudalism—a Catholicism that glorifies slavery." Lastarria noted that ". . . the colonists had been educated precisely to live in servitude and not to desire or even to know a condition better than that to which they had been subjected. Both laws and customs conspired to conceal from their importance and to destroy their individuality. . . ."

The revival or upgrading of Indian culture may be interpreted as a protest against Western religion. It is comparable to a limited brand of anti-Semitism. There are people who believe that much of the current anti-Semitism is a sublimation for some who profess Christianity but who hate Jesus Christ and the ethical tenets of Christianity. Since they hesitate to protest openly against the moral restrictions of the faith and to attack the image of Jesus, they spew their hatred and wrath upon the Jews, who serve as scapegoats and from whose ranks Jesus came, which he never left. In the present day Confederation in Mexico, a call for the revival of Aztec culture is tantamount to a calling for the toppling of Christianity.

The Mexican movement could be picked up easily by the Communists and utilized in various parts of other Latin American states where there are large Indian populations; e.g., Bolivia, Guatemala, Brazil, Ecuador, Peru and Colombia.

The Communists have been working assiduously among the Indian populations of the above-named countries for the past several years. They have been trying to arouse in the Indians a feeling of pride in their ancestry, their ancient culture, and their former status as a free people. The Communists utilize all the injustices, the inequalities, and the third or fourth class citizenship foisted upon the Indians by their white and mestizo superiors. The Communists have not hesitated to go into the jungles, the mountains, and the flat lands to speak to the Indians in their own tongues. They try to create a divisiveness between the Indians and their country-men. These attempts to date have borne little or no fruit because the Communists themselves are either white or mestizos.

Large landholdings, *latifundia,* and haciendas are associated with Spanish colonial rule. They are surviving remnants and an excrescence of Spanish dominion, and serve as reminders of Spain. In Ecuador, at least 400,000 Indians are attached to haciendas as *huasipongos* under a system which keeps them tied to the land (63:188).

It has been said that the Spaniards conquered the New World but that the Indians ultimately conquered the Spaniards. There exist more than traces of the Indian character in the character of Latin Americans. It is important to realize that the Indians have been, at best, only partially assimilated into the cultures of the countries in which they reside. In Mexico, tribes such as the Tarahumara, the Seris, and the Yaqui live in adjacent territories, yet each group lives almost isolated from the other. In Lima, in Iquitos, in Medellin, on the outskirts of Bogotá, in the Zocalo of Mexico City, in Guatemala City, and in La Paz, Indians are still seen in native garb.

The garb of the Indians at Janitizio or Lake Titicaca remains unchanged and unaffected by the styles of mestiza women whom they see and know. It would seem that they are impervious to change. The work done by the Instituto Indigenas Interamericano in Chiapas and the work by UNESCO at Lake Patzcuaro has been in progress for years. The changes wrought by these excellent projects are barely noticeable as one glances at the panorama of Indian Latin America. It will take another two or three generations before there will be a marked, widespread change that will possibly culminate in the passing of whole cultures.

While the mestizo is essentially amoral, the Indian has a double standard. When he is among his own people and community, he dutifully follows the pagan precepts and moral code of his environment. When he lives among the whites or mestizos who fail to treat him as an equal, the Indian too can become amoral, and will rob and cheat and run the gamut of crimes. Neither he nor the mestizo has a sense of shame or feeling of guilt when they violate the laws of those who belittle them.

One wonders at the endurance and strength of the Indians. A steady plodding for four or five hours to the market is a prelude to their weekly few hours of change from their daily routine, for an exchange of words with friends, and for the acquisition of some elementary needs or treats—some overripe bananas, slices of melon or pineapple, colored shaved ices, a piece of roast pig or pork rind, the purchase of a live chicken, a hat, or a *metate*, straw mat, or maté, an herb tea, to be followed by the return home and the passing of six more days until the next market day. The servant girl from the country usually receives only a few hours' respite on Sundays from the obligation to be at the beck and call of the señora.

The weekly hegira of the rural mestizo or Indian to a nearby rural market illustrates the barrenness of their lives and the pitiful extent of their goals, needs, and desires. The rural people bring their goods and produce and sell or barter them for the things that they need. To see them plodding or like ants on the mountainsides of Guatemala making their way to the Chichicastenango market on Thursday or Sunday, carrying tremendous loads on their backs or strapped to their foreheads, brings to mind the trudgings of beasts of burden. The women also carry loads. If the road is open and not beset with low-hanging branches, the loads may be atop their heads. They come literally in colorful thousands. By careful peering through the trees, one can see their stunted bodies walking toward the marketplace soundlessly. There is no chatter, no laugh, no song to break the tedium of a trek that started at three or four o'clock in the morning. "The dominant characteristic of the Indian is a kind of Oriental fatalism" (31A:47).

One of the unique characteristics of all the Indians in Latin America is that each Indian village usually confines its activities for the acquisition of cash to the making of only one product. All the inhabitants of the village make the same kind of thing—pottery, embroidery, or weaving, for instance, permitting individuality only in the design or color details. Another characteristic of Guatemalan and Peruvian Indian villages and those in the Oaxaca valley of Mexico is that women wear blouses with colors characteristic of their villages. This monopolistic use of color and sometimes style by each village facilitates the recognition of the place of residence of the women. In southern Mexico, Central America, and the Peruvian highlands, hats or the trim on the hats and sometimes the style of pants indicate their town and tribe.

The Mexican government has been conscious of the existence of its unabsorbed *indigenistas*. (Peru and Bolivia have not evidenced an equal concern.) The position of the government has been ambivalent. There are many in government circles in each country with an Indian population who wish that these people would just disappear. Attempts to integrate them bear little fruit. When the Otomí, some of whom are known literally as the "Dirt Eaters," were taken from their semidesert land near Ixmiquilpan (125 miles northeast of Mexico City) to fertile regions, they slowly drifted back to their tierra, their land, and their indescribable poverty.

At one time, hundreds of the Yaqui were taken from the barren northwest Mexico to the fertile southeastern part of the country and given land and the implements for farming. Within three years they were all back at the place of origin. The Incas, prior to the coming of Pizarro, used to transport the newly conquered tribes from the periphery of the Inca empire and install them hundreds of miles away in the center of the conqueror's population so that they could be assimilated into the empire. With the downfall of the Incas and the absence of the military restraint, the subject peoples, even after an absence of twenty-five or fifty years from their original domain, returned to it.

This characteristic of strong loyalty and attachment to villages of nativity is matched by the Spaniard. Ramon Menéndez Pidal wrote of the lack of strong national feeling among the majority of Spaniards even in the present century. The place where they were born and reared was their *patria chica*, their small nation. With this they identified and to this place they felt loyalty and patriotism. In Latin America, the rural people, Indian and mestizo, venerate their *tierra*, but particularly the region of their birth, their *pueblito*, the small village. There is no sense of nationalism.

Here we find Spanish and colonial heritage as factors. The *cabildo abierto*, literally an open town council, while not analogous to the New England town meeting, is comparable to it. The *criollo*, native born of white Spanish parents, could aspire to being a *regidor*, councilman, by election, and later when the Spanish kings needed money and sold public office, could buy the position. It was from the town council that the colonists could seek redress, where they could air complaints and participate to some extent in local government affairs. In modern times, it is in their *municipio* that the people can speak up to whatever extent is permitted them.

The town of Alvarado is in the state of Veracruz, whose capital is the city of Veracruz. Alvarado is a prosperous town and bustles with activity. It is on a river where there is commerce and industry. Its schoolchildren use the word "Mexico" for the name of the capital city rather than the name of the country. They feel that the governor of the state of Veracruz is a person whom one respects and fears. The president of the country is a nebulous, distant figure in a place unknown to the inhabitants of Alvarado. How much less is the national feeling of the Indian whose language and culture is non-Spanish.

Frank Tannenbaum has remarked that the mestizo, "a child of conquest, misfortune, denial and contempt" (63:114), emerged after independence but must await a national culture broad enough to embrace all the populace before he can take a full role in the various nations. The fusion of races is stalled until there is "unofficial education in right and good" which is halted because the Indian is voiceless and has the least concept of a nation. The Indian prefers to be left alone to go his own way. The mestizo is apathetic about the status of the Indian and ignores his existence. Tannenbaum proves that "culturally there is no nation," nor national leadership of all the people, until the Indian is integrated into the nation (63:116).

Richard L. Clinton made a study of APRA (Alianza Popular Revolucionaria Americana), the Peruvian sociopolitical movement founded almost forty years ago by Haya de la Torre. In his appraisal of the party, the author reported that the party had jettisoned its earlier dedication to the cause of *indigenismo,* the Indian and his culture, which has not resulted in the loss of any significant support because "of anti-Indian prejudice among mestizos" (9:296).

9 ● Citizenship, Government, and Revolutions

A feature that distinguishes the urban Latin American poor from their counterparts in other places is the degree of the desire to own something. This desire of the Latin American poor is so great that they will acquire even something valueless as long as it is something tangible. A non-Latin might conclude from the knowledge of such great desire by the poor that they would have great respect for property owned by others and by the nation. Yet, one finds no such respect toward property which is publicly owned or any that is not personally theirs. With respect to the property of others, Latin Americans show a degree of concern in accordance with their relationship to the owner thereof. They are most careful of the property of their family, a wee bit less for that of friends, less for that of neighbors and of employers, and then there comes a rapidly declining concern for the possessions of others, the last being that of the impersonal entity of the government.

The individual Latin American sees no connection between public property and himself. That he, as a citizen, has an ownership interest in public buildings, conveyances, or materials is beyond his comprehension. Even in those few countries where there is a withholding tax on his salary, the job holder does not realize that his taxes are used to purchase property which he is defacing, mistreating, or purloining. The gap between himself and the government has not been bridged by the schools or any educational program. Newspapers, as a possible reflection of attitudes of the citizenry, rarely perform public service. They are paid even to publish government health warnings.

Juan Q. Publico is vaguely aware that his taxes pay the emoluments of those on the public payroll, but he regards these people as his superiors. He is subservient to them. There is no concept of civic service or that the basic function and obligation of governmental employees is to serve the public. It is in understanding this attitude concerning the role of public employees that we can begin to comprehend why democracy is not as meaningful to Hispanic Americans as it is to Americans or Englishmen.

It is necessary to understand two widely held concepts. One, which is diminishing, is that might makes right. The man with the gun or the mantle of authority—the army, the police, the bureaucrats—is to be heeded. One does not go to court or elsewhere to seek justice. This partially explains the dearth of tort litigation. One can bribe, pay graft, or render valuable service to bureaucrats to avert a disadvantageous use of power, but one never engages them in combat except in rare cases of desperation or dire need or through inspired riots.

The second concept commonly held is that public employees are the servants of the head of the government. They constitute his personal retinue and, therefore, his position vis-à-vis the public is that of a superior being supplicated in the use of his good offices by the lower or inferior people. The pagan gods had to be appeased by sacrifices, even of life itself. The Church, which assimilated and integrated the pagan deities, required money for its temples and the personal labor and services of its adherents and converts. The Church coffers had to be replenished with silver as the Aztec gods had to be served their daily ration of human blood or the Mayan gods their virgins for their *cenotes,* springs or wells. In comparable manner, the caudillo or cacique is a recipient of whatever one has to give in order to receive favor, protection, or beneficence. This pattern still holds true.

Personalismo describes the governments of Latin America. The charisma of a leader sustains his party. If he does not possess the necessary charisma, the military serves as a means through which the reins of government are retained. Political ideology is of secondary importance. Parties, except MNR, Movimiento Nacional Revolucionario, in Bolivia,* PRI, Partido Revolucionario Institucional, in Mexico, and APRA, Alianza Popular Revolucionario Americana, in Peru, have political strength in direct ratio to the personality of the leader. The facade of congresses and the election of the executive and legislative branches is a manipulated process to support the "election" of a predetermined person as the head of state. The election of Salvador Allende in Chile was an exception to the rule. But the oligarchies—the military, the traditionally wealthy, and the Church—decided that Allende's Marxism was beginning to undermine their *fueros,* rights and privileges, and they toppled him. It must be recalled that Allende had not received a majority of the popular votes— only 30 percent. The head of state is usually called *el presidente.* In most countries, he represents a "fatherhood." Mexico, Paraguay, Nicaragua, and El Salvador are the present prime examples of this attitude.

---

*Bolivia receives scant attention in this book. Marcel Niedergang in his *The Twenty Latin Americas* (The Pelican Latin American Library, English edition, 1971, vol. 2, p. 48) wrote, "Unlike Mexico or Argentina, Bolivia has not suffered the persistent and ridiculous clichés about sombreros, siestas, tangos and comic opera generals. What it has suffered from is total ignorance and from that it suffers still." From 1825 to 1974, Bolivia has had 179 revolutions, which makes it the most turbulent of all Latin American nations.

The Indian title of *cacique* for a chief is synonymous with the Spanish title of *caudillo*. *Cacique* has been incorporated into the Spanish vocabulary in Hispano-America. Although General Franco's title is "El Caudillo," he chooses to translate it as "head of state." A government by a cacique or caudillo is termed *personalismo,* a euphemism for the word "dictatorship." *Caudillismo* or *caciquismo* illustrates another difference among the Latin American nations. This form of government emerged during the nineteenth century after the achievement of independence and is still in existence in some countries. It emerged at different times in different places. Juan Vicente Gómez, who came to power in 1908, was the first real cacique in Venezuela. Argentina had its Juan Manuel de Rosas from 1830 to 1852. Mexico has been under *personalismo* since 1821 even though regimes were called republican, monarchial or democratic. The short regimes of Juarez (1857–1862) and Madero (1910–1912) were exceptions. Some Latin American caudillos have been benign and benevolent and far from being totally corrupt. In Chile, *caudillismo* has made rare and brief appearances between 1830 and 1974. The present military junta is dictatorial.

The emphasis on *personalismo* in politics, plus the tendency of the people to carry over into their political life their veneration of the Virgin and of the saints, have led to the near deification of dictators. In June, 1970, the *Halcones* (Falcons), believed to be police and military disguised in civilian dress, shot and killed and wounded more than 100 Mexican students who were staging a protest march. A few days later President Echeverria convened a mass rally of 100,000 workers in the Zocalo, the large square which formed the center of the city until the nineteenth century. (All workers received a full day's pay from their employers.) There was a twofold purpose: one, to refute rumors that the president was behind the organized acts of the *Halcones;* and second, to rally support for himself by his eloquent appeal to identify the people with him, and vice versa. Scandal-mongers and spreaders of malicious rumors, he intimated, were out to denigrate the holiness of his role as leader of the people.

G. Baez Camargo and Kenneth G. Grubb noted in their book, *Religion in the Republic of Mexico* (p. 27), that ". . . it is beyond doubt a fact that the element of personality still plays a predominant part. The fundamental elements in the caudillo's prestige are not culture, political ideas, or moral character, but the primitive qualities of boldness, astuteness, and even cruelty."

In the nations that had a sedentary Indian civilization, such as Peru, Ecuador, Bolivia, Mexico and Guatemala, the high priest in the precolonial days was also the secular leader. The Indian cacique held both offices. The Aztec Moctezuma (the Nahautl and correct spelling) is an illustration. (He was not the last Aztec emperor. Cuahtemoc, his nephew, was the last emperor.) The Aztecs had permitted local autonomy for all the peoples that they had conquered. They did not incorporate the conquered tribes into their governmental pattern or system. But the Incas did indeed create an empire.

The cacique was all-powerful and could do no wrong. His pronouncements were not questioned by the masses. Licenciado Ramón Beteta was the brilliant editor of *Novedades*, the daily paper with the second largest circulation in Mexico. In a 1964 interview, Beteta was asked why no criticism of the Mexican president ever appeared in the press. He replied that the president was in the same category as the ruling monarch of Great Britain—above any public reproach or criticism. Beteta, as a Mexican, accepted this and saw no incongruity between Mexican democracy and what he had been taught about democracy during the four years that he lived in the United States and studied at the University of Texas.

In 1961, the then Mexican President Adolfo López Mateos gave his annual State of the Union message on September 1. One newspaper reported the following day that the president looked tired toward the end of his three-and-a-half-hour address. This paper was accused of treason by other newspapers because it dared to write that the president appeared tired. Gods are not subject to physical fatigue!

The closer one comes in discussions to the "throne," or to

the seat of the highest official, the more circumspect one must be in voicing opinions in public. This reverence for the person while in office does not bar criticism by the press of officials in the lower echelons. The lower echelons do not include cabinet officials. Cabinet officials in almost all Latin nations are chosen without the consent of any legislative body. They are the alter egos of the president and, therefore, are almost as sacrosanct. Each of them rules his department as did the satraps of old. They are accountable only to the head of the state.

The cabinet members may seek personal publicity, but their official plans, opinions, and projects are never leaked to the press without first securing the consent of the chief. Rumors may run through the capital of what is or is not going to be done, but no public official of the party of *el presidente* would dare to send up trial balloons without authorization of his boss.

A civil service system is a rarity in Latin America. Employment is determined by politics and to the victor belong the spoils. Where there are two parties, or factions, each with relative strength, the victor cannot afford to discharge all public employees for several reasons. In the first place, there is the existence of a high degree of illiteracy in most of the countries of the region, thus limiting the number of qualified personnel. Secondly, among the literate, there are not a sufficient number who would be willing to work for the government at the abysmally low rate of pay. Consequently, there is hardly any change among the bureaucratic employees in the lower posts, even though there may be a change in the political party operating the nation.

Latin American parties and politics present an enigma to North Americans. A prime cause for this enigma is that North Americans insist on making comparisons between their system and that which exists in other states. North Americans are prone to seek analogies. PRI is a national monolithic party in Mexico. It has not lost a national election since 1920. The president, who is the actual head of the party in every sense of the word during his six-year term in office, dictates and controls the naming of his party's nominees for every elective post throughout the country—from mayor of the smallest village to governor of the largest state. While the president may not elect to exercise the power of appointment personally, no person who has earned his displeasure or that of those about him can be nominated. The president appoints the head of PRI and permits the governors of the twenty-nine states to name the party's choices for the state legislatures and for all municipal offices in their territories.

In most countries, there are only national parties with branches throughout the country. These branches possess no autonomy. Our southern neighbors cannot understand how U.S.A. governors or mayors of the same party in office can differ with national policy. The incident of Democratic governors criticizing President Lyndon B. Johnson, a member of their party, in December, 1966, or Republicans disagreeing with President Gerald Ford's policies or taking him to task for not conferring with them on their problems, fills the Latins with amazement. Many compare such actions to anarchy.

With an understanding of the awe that the average citizen in Latin America has for the head of state, we should not be surprised at the average citizen's lack of identification with the president and the property of the state. There is no concept of mutual obligation. The masses are obligated to give, to be subservient, and to obey. The *patrón*, the godhead, the all-wise father, may dispense largesse as he pleases. True, he owes the obligation to provide defense for the citizens in the event of war and to provide some school and educational facilities. Beyond these, he gives all other things out of generosity, because he is good, because he is kind, and because he is *simpático*. In brief, a good president is a benevolent despot.

The Latin American use of public property for political purposes is an abuse only in the eyes of North Americans. The party in power uses all public conveyances, public streets, trees in the parks, and anything available to post its election campaign material. It "subtly" requires all shopkeepers to display its material in store windows. The defacing of public walls and buildings is not considered vandalism by those posting "Yanquis Go Home," or "Cuba Sí, Yanqui No." The signs surreptitiously put on public property are meant as a message to the government because the property belongs to it.

Revolutions

Miguel Jorrin in *Governments in Latin America* differentiates between revolts and revolutions in Latin America (31:183). He wrote that a revolt is the use of force as a means to introduce a change of government—a change in direction or a change of those who direct the government. It does not mean an institutional change. An institutional change results from a revolution—that of Mexico in 1910, and Castro's in Cuba, were the only Latin American revolutions. But, says the professor, a revolt, as does a revolution, calls for the use of force, and it is a negation and antithesis of politics, since politics presupposes the absence of force and violence. His conclusion is that there are too many armed revolts because of the absence of politics and political changes in Latin America. Jorrin here uses "politics and political changes" in the American sense.

Politics is a struggle for power. Political power means control over the conduct of others exercised through governmental institutions. Knowing academically the mechanics of and relationships among these instrumentalities and institutions gives only the picture of a facade or of the superficial veneer of the character of the government and permits labels—e.g., democracy, republican, federal, etc.—to be applied to a particular government. Of greater import, especially in underdeveloped nations, is the pragmatic knowledge of the holder of political power, the manner of attaining the posts of power, and the effects of the utilization of the power.

The loss of individual or family political power in most Latin American countries rarely presents serious economic difficulties. While there are the devastating loss of prestige and the loss of the possibility of doing business with the government, the deposed head usually has "stashed away" sufficient funds in American and Swiss banks to live abroad in quasi-oriental style while awaiting return to power. Peron of Argentina and Perez Jimenez of Venezuela are but two of many examples. The use of the word "family" in the above sentence must be taken in a broader sense than its literal meaning. Frank Brandenburg wrote that Mexico is ruled by an elite and he assigned to this elite the label of "Revolutionary Family" or simply "Family" (6:3).

In the absence of a Latin American comprehension of the significance of orderly changes of government and the reason for such changes being intrinsic to a true democratic system, we should not be surprised at the number of governmental changes wrought by bloodless revolts. Most Latin American revolts are neither social nor egalitarian.

The absence of a widespread sense of nationalism or patriotism, combined with illiteracy which ranges from 50 to 98 percent, produces a feeling of indifference or resignation, rather than national shame, in the overthrow of governments by force or military coups d'état. The only revolution that bore positive fruits is the oft-mentioned Mexican Revolution, whose dates are usually given as 1910–1917. The actual fighting was waged only between 1912 and 1915.

This revolution began without any positive program except that left by the Apostle Francisco Madero, *"Sufragio efectivo, no reeleccion,"* "effective suffrage, no reelection." The cry of Zapata for land and liberty was not echoed throughout the country. The peons and *campesinos* went out in bands to murder and pillage as retribution for the injustices that had been heaped upon them for centuries. These depressed peasants killed the rich, who were nameless and faceless. They hanged and quartered foremen and hacienda storekeepers who had kept them eternally in debt and made them live and work as serfs. They raped and defiled the rich women as retribution for what had been done to their wives and daughters.

Hot blood boiled over with hate and the spice of bitter

gall. To shoot and shoot, to kill and plunder were sufficient ends. The peons did not verbalize what they sought to accomplish. Dr. Mariano Azuela, in his *The Underdogs,* gives a clear and concise picture of the early stages of the Mexican Revolution. The little people fought to topple the government of Porfiro Díaz, who had been deposed in 1910, because his *rurales,* a form of county police, operated as did the more recent Gestapo and S.S. troops.

The *rurales* used to enter a small town on a Sunday and empty the local jail of its weekend drunks and petty thieves. They marched the prisoners to the main street and had them dig a trench of about five feet in depth and long enough to hold all the prisoners standing at arm's length from each other. After the ditch was completed, the prisoners were compelled to stand in it and bystanders were ordered to fill the ditch with the dirt so that all that was left exposed were the heads of the prisoners. Then the *rurales* would line up at the end of the street and race, Cossack-fashion, on horseback down the street. The horses' hooves would crunch the heads of the hapless prisoners while the *rurales* shouted, *"Vivá México, vivá el deporte,"* "hurrah for Mexico, hurrah for the sport."

From the bloodletting of a million Mexicans during the Revolution came the Constitution of 1917, one of the most advanced written instruments of any government. It has stood the test of time and is the document under which Mexico operates. The sentiment of some of the framers of this Constitution was that they were engaged in writing organic laws to weld together heterogeneous peoples and a kaleidoscopic society, but this has yet to penetrate the mentality of much of the populace. The Mexican Constitution, despite its fine wording, is what the current president says it is, and has whatever meaning his supreme court says it has. Luis Echeverria, when he successfully campaigned for the presidency in 1970, kept exhorting, *"La revolución, adelante y arriba!"*— "the Revolution, forward and upward!" Another of his slogans was *"Gobernar es popular,"* loosely translated— "Governments should stimulate population growth." In

February 1975, Echeverria began to back away from this concept.

In some Latin American countries, the overthrow of a government is usually, not necessarily and not always, accompanied by the drafting of a new constitution. The need for such a new document is more apparent than real, for several reasons. In the first place, there is the abyss between promise and deed. The new constitution is only a promise, and there is the ever-present joker in practically every one— the right given to the president to suspend all constitutional liberties and freedoms when, in his opinion, the national welfare requires such suspension. The gap between promise and deed exists in many phases of life. Too often promise and deed are equated. A common Latin American fault is that the potential to do a thing suffices for the deed. This explains the failure to perform a task with full efficiency to complete and successful termination. The rate of concentration upon a task diminishes as the end is in sight.

Constitutions of the Central American republics, in particular, abound with provisions for suspension of all personal guarantees and the rights of the president to legislate when congress is not in session. James L. Busey wrote in *Latin America: Political Institutions and Processes* that "constitutions may not provide a very realistic description of the realities of any governments, least of all those of Latin America" (7:57).

In the second place, the revolution must be justified by the new leaders. Although most of the replacements in positions of power will also pilfer from the national treasury for the benefit of their cohorts, they will, nonetheless, introduce some minor economic reform and other slight improvements in the lot of the downtrodden. Thus, the new constitution becomes a new flag, a new banner and rallying point for the new powers-that-be.

Each new constitution is essentially a rephrasing of the pious protestations of the former and is written to justify to foreign nations the change of government. In some respects, the new constitution is like a check drawn by a deadbeat on a nonexistent bank account. It looks good when it is issued, but heaven help those who attempt to collect on it.

The citizenry of most countries under discussion is wary of the system of justice and even the guarantees under the constitution. Some of these instruments provide for the issuance of a writ of *amparo*. The writ under the Anglo-American system to which it is comparable is the writ of habeas corpus. However, when a person apprehended by the police has been released under *amparo*, usually for forty-eight hours, but capable of extension, the police and all government agencies are barred from molesting him in any manner.

The original purpose for the creation of the writ was commendable. It was devised to protect a candidate for public office from being incarcerated in jail for a lengthy period on some trumped-up charge by an opponent prior to a bitterly-contested election. The writ permitted the accused to continue his campaign and to garner the evidence to disprove the charges leveled against him. Now, even a murderer, if he has sufficient funds and the proper connections and lawyer, may be released. Technically, he can leave the country and no one can stop him.

Recent years have seen "democratically elected" governments overthrown in Peru, Chile, Bolivia, Argentina, Panama and Brazil. It is safe to predict that we shall see, before the end of the decade of 1970, one or two others. The new regimes, usually military, are dictatorships, but with an alleged social concept. However, they are ultimately doomed to topple as predicted by Alfonso Lopez Michelsen, son of the former President Lopez of Colombia, "The right to be wrong is a principle inadmissible both in the Roman Catholic Church and in a totalitarian state." Lopez Michelsen is a Roman Catholic and professor of constitutional law.

Trade Unionism

On January 12, 1971, labor leaders from all Latin American nations met in Mexico City. George Meany and other

American notables came to extend greetings to the conference which was to mark "Twenty Years of Free Trade Unionism in America." Many speeches were made and pertinent remarks about the state of labor unions in Latin America were uttered. Most are not germane to this chapter except for some comments made by Julio Cruzado, secretary general of the Peruvian CTP. He stated that he and other labor leaders "are filled with horror by the knowledge and proof that men of the cloth . . . are fighting . . . carrying in one hand the cross that redeems men and in the other the hammer and sickle that enslaves them. . . . The defect of our democracies is the dishonesty of those who practice it, and licentiousness and immorality."

I have quoted the above because I believe that if the power of the unions increases with the passing of the years and with the increases in industrialization, a new brand of revolution will appear in Latin America. It will be a workers' revolution led by those who use the word "democracy" but whose understanding of the freedoms implicit in it are not within their purview of the word. This is illustrated by the statement that "the gravest defect of our democracy [Peruvian style] is that it tolerates within its bosom elements who do not know and do not want to understand the meaning of a true democracy with liberty and justice."

10 ● Universities, Schools, and Students

In the word *universidad,* "university," we again find differing concepts. In English, the word is defined as an educational institution of the highest level with one or more undergraduate schools or colleges together with a program of graduate studies and a number of professional schools, authorized to confer various degrees ranging from the baccalaureate to doctor of philosophy.

Latin American universities fostered concepts of independence toward the latter part of the nineteenth century. When the struggle between conservatives and liberals, between federalists and centralists broke out after independence, the universities spawned the political leaders and often the leaders of society. The universities became integral units and the rectors possessed powerful political influence.

In 1918, a movement, "University Reform," began in Cordoba, Argentina, met with success and began to sweep across all of Latin America. The students, joined by a few faculty members, revolted against the antiquated system and the establishment. The revolutionaries sought a broadening and liberalizing of curriculum to include more social and physical sciences. They demanded a voice in the administration of the university.

This opened the door to the entry of the student body into the politics of the country. One of the results of the reform movement was a broadening of admission policies (although not a lessening of academic admission requirements) so that those of the lower social and economic classes could enter. In some countries, attention began to be paid to the welfare of the communities with the result that closer contact between university and general public was fostered.

Latin American universities, including student life, are patterned on those of Europe. The universities comprise only graduate or professional schools. Their degrees begin with a licentiate (considered by Latins as equivalent to our master's degree except for economists and lawyers) and go on to include various doctorates. Most of these universities include a lower school, the *preparatoria*. This is a combination of our senior high school and the approximate equivalent of the first year of junior college. Its graduates receive a bachelor's title, *bachillerata*, which is not held in high regard. In Cuba, a law student receives a doctorate after three years of law school.

Because the *preparatorias* are under the aegis of the national university, their student body is included in the enrollment numbers of the university. Consequently, many Latin American university registration figures are misleading and are not comparable to American university statistics. If we included our secondary school or senior high school registration with that of our colleges, the total would be astronomical compared to Latin American schools of higher learning. The National Autonomous University of Mexico (UNAM) claimed a student body in 1969 in excess of 85,000. However, over 45,000 are students in the *preparatorias* and almost 12,000 are *en pasante* — those who have finished the course work for the doctorate, but have not written their dissertation. These people frequently feel that their status is equivalent to that of those actually holding the doctorate, and consequently, use the title. Some completed their course work more than fifteen years ago, but they are still carried on the student roster and many remain active in student political activities. This swollen enrollment permits a request for a larger annual budget, creates a political force within the university, and has led to certain abuses. Salvador de Madariaga reports that in the Law Faculty of the University of Buenos Aires, 20,000 are registered as students, but only 8,000 are in attendance (39:13).

The national universities have different "careers," fields of study. Each is an independent unit, and it is almost impossible for a student of one "career" to take courses in another. For example, an engineering student cannot, except through influence, take a course in the humanities. The faculty of history and philosophy accepts only its own students for its course of study or "career." All courses are required and there are few, if any, electives which may be added.

There are about 120 universities in the twenty-three Latin American nations, about 100 of which are national and state universities. The Jesuits run several universities and there is less than a handful of nonsectarian, private universities. Most of the teachers work on a part-time basis (35:3). Full-time instructors constitute about 20 percent of the total. Only 3 percent of the Latin American universities have a full roster of full-time professors. Campus life is practically nonexistent, and dormitories are the exception rather than the rule. Participation in sports is confined to a minority, and athletic events, except soccer, are few. Intramural sports are unknown and international competition is rare.

There is another cognate word that has a different meaning in English than in Spanish. In English a professor is one who teaches on the college or higher level. Except for a few South American countries, a *profesor* in Hispano-America is a teacher in an elementary or secondary school or in a *preparatoria*. In the *universidades*, we have a *maestro* (master plumbers, carpenters, head engineers, etc., are also called *maestro)* or *catedratico*. A *colégio* is not a college. It is any school below that of a university and includes grades from kindergarten through secondary school. Ellwyn R. Stoddard has been engaged at the University of Texas at El Paso in comparative studies of attitudes and images of Mexican and U. S. university students. He reports that even common terminology such as "natural sciences" *(ciencias naturales)* "had *no* meaning for the foreign student." He theorizes that "difficulties might cause some doubt as to whether U. S. scholars can give valid interpretive meanings to materials from Latin American countries without having a thorough knowledge of the structural-functional variations and cultural distinctions between those researching and those researched" (62:486). This writer would change doubt to certainty, and therefore deplores the waste of literally millions of dollars by American universities and our government in making surveys abroad.

Except for Dr. Ignacio Chavez of Mexico, I know of no other university rector who has attempted to purge the student roster of nonstudents or of those who perennially fail their examinations. Dr. Chavez was compelled to write his resignation at midnight in April, 1966, under the gunpoint threat by students that he would be tarred and feathered unless he did. In 1959, Nabor Carillo Flores, then rector, told Adlai Stevenson and Senator William Benton that he had held office for seven years, but eleven of his predecessors had had an average service of one year and ten months, and that three had resigned because of threats of physical violence to be administered by students. Changes in rectors are still frequent in most Latin American universities and invariably occur when a government falls.

All national universities south of the border, except Brazil, have governing councils with student representation. They are patterned on the thirteenth-century Bologna type of university. This consists of a cooperative student-faculty council, with the students active in the employment of the professional staff. The councils are composed of the deans of the various schools, and usually one faculty member and one student from each school. The students are permitted to bring alternates. The councils elect boards of governors who select the rector (equivalent to a chancellor or president in U. S. A.) who is either nominated openly or suggested secretly by the president of the nation.

The student representation often opens the door to built-in anarchy. Standards set under student pressure are low. In some schools passing grades can be bought; rumors of examinations being sold are common. Student privileges are inviolate. The professional or perpetual students, often men between thirty and fifty years of age, use the students as political pawns, and the campuses become training grounds for political activity.

Under Spanish colonial rule, the universities of San Marcos at Peru, Mexico City, and Santo Domingo were awarded the earliest charters. Theology, rhetoric, law, and Latin were the principal courses. Later philosophy and medicine were added. The sciences formed no part of the curriculum. The faculties were members of the clergy, principally Dominicans and Jesuits. The Church in those days was a sanctuary into which neither the police nor army dared to enter in order to apprehend a criminal. This concept of the campus as a sanctuary has been carried over to the present autonomous universities.

For forty years, with one exception, the autonomy was respected in every country. The practice of autonomy and the loose organization within the universities have permitted political parties to infiltrate the campuses. Political agitators find a haven from arrest on the university grounds.

In the United States, the goal in college is to teach students to reason, to use their minds, to motivate them to independent study and research. In most Latin American educational systems, memory or response by rote is the key to success.

Despite a general concept fostered by careless American news reporting, the autonomous universities are not hotbeds of Communism. It is true that some departments of a university have Marxist or Communist directors and faculty members. In such departments, usually those of economics, political science, and sociology, a student can be "brain-washed" with Marxism and socialism during a four- or five-year stay. Only those strong of will and with outside offsetting influences can complete their studies with relatively free minds. On the other hand, there are departments of the humanities, such as history and philosophy, where the major influence may be that of conservatism, and, at times, church dogma. It is, therefore, inaccurate to generalize too readily about Communism in the universities.

Communists believe in active, strong, vocal minorities, and these exist on every campus. Their sound and fury are often out of proportion to their numerical strength and influence. They also can rally masses with money. In Latin America, mob demonstrators are available for a pittance. In Guatemala, Colombia, Mexico, and Chile, students will attend protest meetings for the equivalent of fifty cents without even knowing or caring about the nature of the protest. Despite journalistic reports to the contrary, there is no such thing as a spontaneous mob. Each Communist student leader has his corps of non-Communists who will rally to his call upon the promise of the fixed stipend.

Many of the students are often maneuvered by their leaders into taking action. In the three-month anarchy that reigned at the Mexican National University from February to May, 1966, the leadership came from the *Facultad de Leyes* (Law School), where the uprising originated. The general student body did not know at the outset exactly for what they were fighting. (No student lost any credit or time, although classes were not held for three months. No student leader was disciplined, although physical damage to University property and equipment in three *preparatorias* ran over a million pesos.)

Student leaders appear to be a combination of opposites: intelligent, yet illogical and hot-blooded; idealistic and cynical; pro- as well as anti-Church. Many of them drop classes because they believe that their role in politics will improve their country's social, economic, and political situation. The intellectual elite senselessly destroys and defaces public buildings as well as their own laboratories, libraries, and other physical facilities.

When student movements have been involved in national politics, the following appears to be the general pattern. First, the students attribute the shortcomings of their country to inept, corrupt governmental officials. Second, either protests are inserted in newspapers or marches to public offices are made. Then comes the inevitable storm. When political factions are in conflict and censorship or curfews or both are imposed, the students use the sanctity of the campus of the autonomous university to flaunt any decrees of the police or other authorities.

Strikes and demonstrations are often the first steps taken by the students who cut classes, march and hold meetings at the Zócalo or other main city plaza which is the center of every Latin American city. They ignore regular legal procedures to seek a redress of wrongs, feigned or real. The resort to proper channels is derided because the students feel that the powers-that-be are corrupt and inefficient. The students, as well as their elders, have little confidence in the administration or dispensation of justice. Their motto might be, "Create disorder and then resort to violence to right the wrong." A not uncommon occurrence is the seizure of a public bus or buses, and holding it or them if compensation for the death of a student as the result of a bus accident has not been agreed upon or paid as rapidly as it should be. When students object to increases in fares on public conveyances on routes that they use, they will set fire to buses including those that might be municipally owned.

Luis Alberto Sanchez, former rector of the University of San Marcos in Peru, characterized the Latin American student as a young person dissatisfied with the society in which he lives, with the way in which he is developing as an individual, and with the means available for him to achieve his objectives. Consequently, he is dominated by the desire to protest against the injustice which he feels binds him, and he is impelled to rebel against those forces which he thinks are blocking his goals (58). (For an amplification and further elucidation of many of our comments on Latin American students and universities, read *Student Politics in Chile* [5].)

The orientation of many Latin American universities is to the prestigious professions. Most young men desire careers in law, engineering, or architecture. Economics rates near the top because it is an open door to government employment. Careers in the humanities, such as teaching, philosophy, and history, are neglected. Despite the idealism of the students, they aspire to material success or power and seek those careers which will provide either in the shortest time.

During the past few years, four autonomous university campuses have been raided by government forces. This occurred in Argentina, Mexico, Venezuela, and Colombia. In Venezuela, arms and munitions were found, graves of Communists who had been killed by the police were uncovered, and a Communist headquarters revealed. This does not mean that all the students were Communists or even Communist supporters. It does, however, mean that among non-Communist students, loyalty to the principle of the sanctity of university grounds was greater than loyalty to their country and to law and order. Presidents Leoni of Venezuela and Onangia of Argentina have, tacitly in one case and explicitly in the other, stated that the principle of autonomy was subordinate to the government's obligation to maintain peace and order and administer the law in every foot of the country. This is a bitter pill for university students to swallow.

In Mexico, President López Mateos and the government stood by in 1964 while the National University and *preparatoria* laboratories were destroyed, buildings (including the famous Casa de la Inquisición) were defaced, buses overturned, molotov cocktails thrown, etc. Whether governmental inertia was due to ulterior motives is a question that remains unanswered. (In 1968, President Díaz Ordaz broke precedent in entering the grounds of University City and stationing the army and riot police. One must recall that the Olympic games were in the offing and the government feared that the student violence would keep tourists away, and disrupt the games.)

In October, 1966, Mexican federal troops were sent into the campus of the University of Morelia in the State of Michoacan. Here Communist-led students had organized a drive to overthrow state Governor Agustin Arriaga Rivera because the students blamed him for the accidental death of a student in a demonstration. That the student demonstrations in Morelia were Communist-inspired and directed under plans or orders emanating from Fidel Castro seems quite evident.

However, between the 1966 troubles at the National University in Mexico City and that of Morelia there was the incident of the students in the State of Durango taking over an iron mine and defying 10,000 federal troops in June, 1966. It was charged that this was an action inspired by foreigners seeking to weaken government authority. One is prompted to believe that the Mexican government finally moved in October, not so much because of the charge that foreigners were interfering in Mexican political affairs, but because the public and the conservative press had assailed past government attitudes and excessive respect for autonomy principles. (One learns in Latin America that the obvious, or self-evident, is too often not the motivation for action. One must judge by hindsight. Ultimately, President Díaz Ordaz removed the state governor for failure to uphold the law and to enforce order.)

The Latin trait of seeking to place blame on others and attributing culpability to outside forces was revealed in blatant fashion in Mexico after the heinous events of the *Halcones* on June 10, 1970. Several prominent Mexicans stated that foreign powers (many clearly implying the U.S.A.) were the fomenters of the tragic occurrences.

To Americans it may seem an unprecedented, if not abusive, act for a president summarily to remove the elected governor of a state. This, however, is within the authority and power of the Mexican presidency, as well as other presidents. Lic. Adolfo López Mateos summarily removed three or four state governors during his regime (1958–1964), and his predecessor, Ruiz Cortines, did the same. The president can remove an elected official without trial or hearing (with no impeachment proceedings of any kind) — and then appoint a successor to serve the unexpired term of the man removed. One must read the fine print in some Latin American constitutions to fathom the significance of what they include under so-called democratic processes. The president of Argentina has somewhat similar powers of removal. In many countries, presidents can appoint "intervenors" to take over a business, a factory, a labor union or any arm of the government. Allende and the present military junta which overthrew him in Chile and Velasco in Peru have made numerous uses of this provision.

In October, 1966, Colombian police had to invade the campus at Bogotá because the Communist-controlled "Federation of Students" hurled rocks, tomatoes, rotten eggs and insults at President Carlos Lleras Restrepo and U.S. financier John D. Rockefeller III when they arrived at the University to open an agricultural course sponsored by the Rockefeller Foundation. The seething unrest found among students is universal in our days. The primary difference is one of degree, but the results of this unrest vary greatly. Some U. S. university students ape their southern counterparts.

We must interpolate here a significant point developed by James L. Payne in *Patterns of Conflict in Colombia* (46: passim). Payne rejects the notion that Colombia's politicians can be meaningfully divided into "left" and "right" and conservative or liberal. Power and status are most highly desired, and party affiliations are used to acquire status. There is no commitment to a party platform. A play to the masses to achieve personal ends will be made even if detrimental to the nation. Olien writes that groups identified with reform seek access to power as an end in itself (45A: 103) Students ape their political leaders. Payne wrote, "To understand the turbulent politics of Colombia, one must first discover what motivates Colombian politicians."

In Latin America where social justice is a crying need

and the problems of the poor and the imbalance between agriculture and population growth constitute national problems, one finds few student bodies interested in these aspects of life. The neglect of the educational process in inculcating civil responsibility and a concern with welfare plus inadequate educational goals and inferior and unrealistic teaching, leaves the field open for Communist agitators. Let it be said that at times Latin students do demonstrate and act politically to instigate revolt against dictators.

The "University Reform Group" in Panama has been infiltrated by Communists. Two F.R.U. leaders were each given $75.00 to attend the Latin American Student Congress in Havana. This was a follow-up of the Tri-Continental Conference in January, 1966, in Havana. These trips, which are intended for indoctrination of student representatives, should be contrasted with the aims of the United States in its student exchange program. Dr. E. R. Stoddard, sociologist at the University of Texas, wrote in 1969 anent bicultural relations that they occur, at least between the U.S. and Mexico, because "the Mexican representatives have deferred to the values and informal demands of the American influentials on a near unilateral basis" (62:485). He concluded that most Cultural Understanding Weeks and Good Neighbor programs are conducted as a facade to hide the social and cultural processes across the border which Americans do not understand and are even less concerned about.

While schools of engineering, medicine, dentistry, and architecture have few vacancies, many students choose law so that they can become apprentice politicians. Per capita, there are more employees with law degrees on Latin American governmental payrolls than in any other place in the world. The title *licenciado,* usually signifying a law degree or one in economics, is highly prized and is the key to government administrative posts. The holder may be addressed only as "Licenciado," as many Americans use the title "Doctor" when the person addressed is an M.D.

Many university graduates serve as part-time instructors and lecturers. While the pay is poor, the title is prestigious. Latin American governments reward men of culture. A recognized historian is frequently put on a government payroll as press director or some other innocuous post, and a popular faculty member is assured of a government sinecure. His sole obligation is to sign the payroll and collect his check monthly, or semimonthly. As one of these gentlemen told me in South America, he is an *aviador;* he "flies" in to the government office twice a month for his paycheck.

In Central America and Chile, the governments and university administrations have recognized publicly their shortcomings. This confession, unheard of historically, was followed up by appeals to some American university heads to lend experienced administrative and educational leaders so that the universities could be thoroughly overhauled. What is happening in Central America must be repeated in all other countries, and until this occurs, our educational and cultural exchange programs will be sadly deficient and almost self-defeating.

American universities feel that they must have foreign students and foreign visiting professors. American schools feel that they must have an international program and that their campuses should represent not so much a cross-section of the United States, as a cross-section of international students. Even at the University of Miami, Dr. Henry King Stanford boasted in his annual report for 1966 that his school has over 1000 students from foreign lands out of an approximate total full-time student body of 12,000. We also feel that we must have our professors serve abroad. President Sterling of Stanford University expressed a concern about reducing our own number of educators to the point of over-commitment to foreign schools resulting in the "jet set professor" to whom our students can talk only on the way to the airport.

Then there is the American "need" for a "junior year abroad." Having taught abroad and having had a unique opportunity to know and observe American students at more than one foreign university, I feel that this kind of program offers some benefits, but generally is greatly abused and overrated. At least one of our cultural attachés has expounded on this subject and astounded his audience in Texas with similar opinions. Dr. John Brown discussed Stephen Freeman's Study of Consultative Service on U. S. Graduate Study Abroad, in which he reported that the alarming proliferation, the duplication of effort, and, in certain cases, the academic illegitimacy of study abroad threatens to become a national educational scandal. There are approximately 30,000 students engaged in these programs each year. In three Mexican and two Central American universities, students attending summer courses are exposed to subtle Communist and anti-American propaganda. One professor at the Mexican National University, in 1964, had the temerity to state that the U.S.A. was exploiting Puerto Rico and depressing the population. When a mature American woman student violated his rule against asking questions in class and asked him when he was last in Puerto Rico, he replied that he had never been there.

Studying must compete with the distractions of foreign surroundings and attractions. Furthermore, students, like most people, have a tendency to associate with those of similar ethnic roots. Too often the students at foreign universities are not given any orientation to the new culture. They are thrust into a foreign culture and environment, and, in self-defense, they seek their own kind. Many mature students, as do some travelers, come away with little other than curios and souvenirs, a list of restaurants and hotels, accounts of encounters with a handful of foreigners, and incidents involving the unexpected meeting of people from their own town and state.

Adolescents are no different from their elders. They haven't the apperceptive capacity or the preparation or basis for a fruitful understanding of a foreign culture. We repeat an apt adage that "to discover the wealth of the Indies, we must take the wealth of the Indies with us." Exchange programs for postgraduate students are usually profitable because of their maturity, professional interest, and some prior knowledge of the language and culture of the country visited.

On the other side of the coin, we must consider the foreign student coming to the States. Many who arrive from Latin America are inadequately prepared and are incapable of meeting the standards of American graduate schools. Many of the leaders of our cultural exchange programs admit the deficiencies of the students, but they feel that exposure to our country, our democracy, our affluence, will make them friends of our country and cause them to encourage emulation of us at home. It usually results in an opposite effect.

The director of the leading computer center in a Latin American country (a Communist whose political affiliation was most tardily learned by the C.I.A. and our State Department) has been a frequent visitor to our land. He is perfectly bilingual and has been trained in the United States. He summarized the reactions of many Latin Americans when he said, "I am capable of being a cosmopolite when I am a visitor in your country or any other. I can see all the advantages that you have over other nations, and I profit by being there. However, when I fly home to my own country, and I land at our airport, all your culture rolls off my back and I am a pro-_____ [naming his country]. I am no better and no worse than my countrymen, and their prejudices and biases are my prejudices and biases." The ex-dictator of Colombia, Gustavo Rojas Pinillo, attended an American college in his youth, but he was no lover of democracy.

There are many Latin American graduate students who fail to make the grade in American universities. Do they return home and cite their own failures to study or their inadequate preliminary training as the causes of their debacle? No! They attribute their return (unsuccessful experience) to North American prejudice and unfairness. The article by Larrea in *Cuadernos Americanos* (January, 1965), an outstanding scholarly quarterly, corroborates this.

The returning defeated student is inwardly bruised and bitter, and he will confirm any and all anti-gringo statements made in his presence and add his own. Salvadore de Madariaga commented that there is an intense anti-American feeling, particularly among students and professors, as well as the professional classes. This antipathy may flow from frustrating experiences in contacts with their American counterparts (40:14). (In the Argentinian epic poem, *Martin Fierro,* there is the line, "How bad and ugly is the gringo" (54:24).)

The evaluation of Latin American degrees heretofore mentioned (some of those from Cuba's University of Havana are below par for Latin America) will wound and exacerbate the pride of Hispano-American universities. They should be told that our master's degree is superior and represents more quality learning than their *licenciado* and that their doctorate is not the equivalent of our Ph.D. Leapold Zea, as the dean of the Faculty of Humanities of Mexican National University, laid down a rule effective in 1968, that an earned degree of *maestria* has to be attained between the *licenciado* and *doctorado.*

Dr. John Brown, the distinguished former U. S. cultural attaché previously mentioned, said that he feels that we are guilty of a quantitative heresy. We are always striving to make things bigger in the hope that they will automatically be better; but this does not work in the realm of educational exchange. He put it nicely, "Here, as in all the arts, it very often happens that less is more." Latin Americans who visit the United States of America return with great admiration for American techniques but with little comprehension of the society in which these techniques operate. Many also fail to realize that American culture is organized around the attempt at active mastery, rather than passive acceptance.

There are other returnees who leave our land with envy and jealousy. They were overwhelmed by our libraries, our facilities, our laboratories, and our affluence. The gap between what is here and what they have at home is so great that despair sets in and they make no attempt to change conditions because the magnitude of the task thrusts defeat upon them. Those who admit our technical, industrial, and economic achievements marvel at such accomplishments from "cultural barbarians." These people sincerely believe that Latin America is the sole repository of genuine human value. The students come here with prejudices and few lose them while many acquire new ones. André Gide is quoted by Dr. Brown as having said, "What's the use of exchanging ideas? I'd rather keep my own." This form of chauvinism is typical of Latin Americans.

There are exchanges which can and do serve excellent purposes. These exchanges are of teen-agers who exchange homes for periods ranging from ten weeks to six months. When they live with a family as a member of the family, the odds for success are vastly improved. These programs are called "Operation Amigo."

A prominent American historian once said that the history of Mexico consists of legends with footnotes. Octavio Paz, a Mexican, and Julia Cortazar, an Argentinian, both utilize their literary efforts as a revolt against "historical abstraction" according to Carlos Fuentes. (Fuentes is now the Mexican ambassador to France.) He states that "in Latin America, fantasy *is* history. History as change does not exist; there is only the compulsive repetition of ritual acts. The Latin American is forced to face nothing before anything." We might add that since the great majority of the population is rural, they, like most rural peoples, are reluctant to accept change. They cling with fervor to mores and behavior patterns which provide security in situations which do not reveal their inadequacies.

The poverty of university life in many of the countries is evidenced by the presence of so many of their intellectuals in countries other than their own — expatriates. The rather long list of these voluntary exiles is headed by Ruben Dario, Latin America's greatest poet, and Silvio Zavala, a great historian. Many others elect to serve for many years in the diplomatic corps or in other capacities as long as they do not have to live in their native lands. Others, such as Octavio Paz, were given posts abroad because some of the powers-that-be fear the words and thought of some of the most enlightened. Can the urge to reside elsewhere be due to the awareness of the cultural shortcomings and of the stifling university life of their own nations or that no man is a prophet in his own land?

All private schools are under strict government supervision. Several directors of private schools, from primary to university, have stated that the government schools would be much better if the government inspectors spent as much time in these schools as they do at the private institutions. In some of the countries, fear of the Church is the reason for the close attention, which, while aimed at the parochial schools, must be made to appear impartial so that all schools come under close scrutiny.

Uniform textbooks, uniform curriculum, and, as in Uruguay, a single uniform for pupils of all schools, are considered necessary for implanting love of country and nationalistic fervor. Uniforms vary in each country. Most schools have their own pattern or color scheme. Private schools have a complete uniform: sweater, blouse or shirt, pants or skirt, and socks. The public schools in the poor areas require only a blouse or sweater. The Uruguayan requirement for all children in all schools to wear the same white for girls and khaki for boys breeds a concept of democratic equality.

As of 1970 there were over fifty American elementary and secondary schools in Latin America, subsidized in part by the United States. They had an enrollment of 20,000 pupils in elementary and secondary grades, of which two-thirds were Latin American or of other than American nationality (45:173 for pre-1970 figures). This abuse of American taxpayers' monies is little known. It is defended by our diplomatic corps because it provides a form of patronage for them. They can secure admission for children of influential people in the countries to which they are assigned. These schools are private institutions and are used by the children of wealthy foreigners who can thus secure a bilingual education.

The proliferation of law students and lawyers has failed to breed respect for the law. In Mexico, "lawyer" and "coyote" are almost synonymous.

Universities have immense stadia. Soccer is the national game. Sportsmanship, American-style, is a rarity — especially for the spectators. Latins take their sporting events seriously — which is beyond cavil. However, many Latins are poor losers. Sports provide an outlet for their emotions. It serves as catharsis. In 1964, in Lima, Argentina was playing soccer against Peru. The winner was to represent Latin America at the next Olympic games. In the last minute of the game, the umpire, a Uruguayan, disallowed a goal, thereby making Peru the loser instead of winner. A Peruvian spectator ran onto the field with a broken bottle to attack the umpire. As crowds followed him, the police rushed to save the umpire and the Argentinian team; the mob then turned against the police; the gates were closed, and 319 corpses were the result. Georgie Ann Geyer notes that during the fighting, "a common hatred of the police erupted" (19:28). In the subsequent investigation to seek the causes, the result was that the fault lay with the Uruguayan umpire, a foreigner, who had ruled against Peru. He was the "intellectual author" of the massacre. Similar tragedies occurred in Mexico in 1968 in the pre-Olympic games. As a result of the 1970 World Cup games in Mexico City, four murders were blamed on arguments over the World Cup, and several hundred were arrested for stealing and rowdy behavior. Wild jubilation over victories was caused by *"wrongly based nationalism . . . childishness . . . and Latin temperament,"* according to the psychiatrist, Luis Haro Leeb.

11 ● Nationalism, Xenophobia, and Chauvinism

The achievement of independence for almost all of the countries of Latin America (Cuba and Panama being notable exceptions) during the second decade of the nineteenth century did not awaken immediately a sense of nationalism among the masses of people in the new sovereign states. Among the factors that impeded the spirit of nationalism was the hacienda (45A:102). The *haciendados* retained local and economic control for over a century, in most instances until the 1930's.

The political leaders of the nations were satisfied to rule through the oligarchies and local chieftains and any others who held local power. The spread of mass communication, especially the radio; the impetus to build roads, aided by American funds; the automobile; public transportation; and the aeroplane finally brought a considerable part of the rural populations into the mainstream of national life. The League of Nations, too, contributed to a consciousness of nationhood. Each of the Latin American countries began to feel that, through membership, it was part of a larger family of nations. Although it involved only minimally the Latin American countries (except Argentina as friend of Germany), World War II heightened the awareness of nationhood. Finally, the formation of the United Nations brought realization of the necessity of developing citizens who would be aware of national identity, loyalty and patriotism. The urbanization of Latin America and its concomitant industrialization contributed to the "rise of nationalism as the dominating and unifying political ideology . . ." (45A:282).

Modern Latin American society appears to be an amalgam of complexities and paradoxes. There are revolutions and stability (stability, in this context, meaning the retention of the traditional status quo with some social progress); nationalism and regionalism, which was a continuation of the earlier battle of federal power versus regional power; and the search for a brand of economics that is not capitalism, communism or Marxian socialism.

Claudio Veliz wrote (65:1), "In spite of its reputation for frequent and violent political upheaval, perhaps the principal contemporary problem of Latin America is excessive stability. There exists in the region a resilient traditional structure of institutions, hierarchian arrangements and attitudes which condition every aspect of political behavior and which have survived centuries of colonial government, movements for independence, foreign wars and invasions, domestic revolutions and a confusingly large number of palace revolts."

Now, nationalism has become the clarion call of all governments. Everyone must be ostentatiously nationalistic. The members of the oligarchies, big business, and the middle sector echo the cry similar to that frequently heard in our own country, "America for Americans." South of the border it is *"Peru para los Peruanos"* or *"Panama para los Panameños."*

In the name of nationalism in some Latin American countries, foreign enterprises are nationalized or, at least, a majority of the shares must be owned by citizens or the government, and areas for foreign investment are curtailed.

Many large companies or individual industrialists no longer want foreign partners or investors.

They are on the horns of a dilemma. While they desire modernization and the benefits of foreign funds and technology, they have come to feel that many North American companies are challenging the sovereignty of their nation by attempts to secure benefits for themselves and attempts to interfere in the government decision-making processes. (45A:235). The large industrialists and the oligarchies are also perturbed by a loss of political power to the middle sector. They feel that the loss of such power will be ruinous economically to the country. This middle sector is tied to traditional perspectives. In Chile, according to James Petras in his book, *Politics and Social Forces in Chilean Development* (48), the tradition-bound middle sector is largely responsible for Chile's economic strangulation, as well as the failure to fully integrate the lower social strata. This failure was capitalized on by Allende in his campaign for the presidency. However, Allende's Marxist programs did not succeed in improving conditions.

The rural masses are not yet in the mainstream of the country. They are still rigidly parochial. Parochialism in Latin America has fostered the distrust of all foreigners. The rural mestizo and the Indian who is sufficiently cognizant of the areas beyond his locale will, therefore, join in any movement which appeals to their parochialism. The others who are illiterate and unconcerned with anything beyond their family or locale follow sheep-like the dictates of their *patrón* or *jefe politico*.

By trumpeting nationalism and the call for national enterprises—e.g., *Venezuela para los Venezuelanos*, etc.—the large entrepreneur hopes to prevent the rise of Communism. He knows that the political forces will enact protective tariffs, will ensure monopolistic practices for him, and will curtail the rights of foreign investors and firms as long as he plays the politicians's game of nationalism.

Sovereignty is to a nation what liberty is to an individual. Just as each individual desires to exercise his liberties within lawful restraints, so sovereign states want to pursue their national, especially internal, policies without caustic comments, preaching, or teaching from other states. Among the aspects of sovereignty highly prized by underdeveloped and developing nations is the respect of outsiders for their culture. There is a craving for foreigners to give public recognition to their development. Nations, like individuals, which have inferiority complexes, make demands for recognition in order to bolster their pride and self-respect.

Inferiority complexes induce the holders thereof to seek scapegoats upon whom they can place blame and to supply excuses for their shortcomings. The blame must all be laid at the doors of others. Only the strong and the intellectually honest can bear their inadequacies and shoulder blame. Chauvinism evidences itself in many ways in Latin America. The most common are the many restraints on the rights of foreigners to find employment, the length of stay, the requirements for visas, visa photos, the calling for nationals to be the first to go through customs and other burdensome red tape at international airports on the arrival of planes from abroad.

Mexico has a rare provision in its constitution. Only a native-born person both of whose parents are Mexican-born is eligible for nomination for the presidency. This may be seen as a relic of the Spanish Inquisition's demand for *limpieza de sangre*, "purity of [Catholic] blood," for eligibility to an official post. Of course, the Inquisition disqualified all New Christians. Only Old Christians, for four generations, had the necessary purity of blood.

Salvador de Madariaga, Spanish liberal, statesman, and scholar, wrote in 1961 that in Latin America, "liberal democracy" was being jeopardized because of exposure to the hazards of inexperience and "of a more vigorous than intelligent nationalism." He deplored the growth of national independence under circumstances which are not contributing to stable order (39:14).

One of the harshest comments made on Latin American nations came from Madariaga. He says that these nations suffer from a sense of frustration and a "feeling of hurt pride and of injustice undergone." This makes public opinion more emotional than elsewhere, and these emotions are polarized against the Colossus of the North.

> A score of weak nations, poor in the midst of their natural resources, scattered over huge territories, heirs to a powerful and colorful past, but divided by nature and character, struggling to raise themselves to the status they think theirs by natural right, look with impatience, and at times with resentment, on the power, wealth and success of a *parvenu* nation which was still uncouth and rustic when they were already civilized. [39:2]

Madariaga terms them a "motley crowd of nations with little or no international weight," and he adds that few of their men attain world fame, few of their literary figures enjoy international readers, and few of their statesmen attain a reputation other than that which courtesy or convenience suggests. The Latin American nations, as did the Jews for 2000 years, feel that they are objects rather than subjects of history. Things happen or are done to them and they are impotent to generate events or actions.

Events in the United Nations have further induced a sense of frustration, and, subconsciously, a sense of ineptitude. For the first five years of the existence of the U.N., the Latin American bloc (although it was not a real bloc since they rarely voted as a bloc (75:66), constituted 40 percent of the members of the U.N. They were twenty-one nations out of a total of fifty-one. Now they are not even considered a bloc, and since Cuba is Communist and, therefore, not counted, and Haiti rarely attends, they are nineteen out of 152, or less than 7 percent. Many Latin American nations are in default in the payment of assessments to various U.N. agencies or forces, including "local cost" operations of U.N. technical assistance projects which they requested (75:68). They see no inconsistency between voting for the incurring of obligations to the U.N. and the failure to pay for the obligations.

Arrears to the U.N. are more than matched by arrears to the Organization of American States (O.A.S.). The *Miami Herald* of April 28, 1971, reported that the U.S. had "to pay an extra 10 million dollars towards financing the O.A.S., because many Latin members were 'chronically' behind on their dues. . . ." (The O.A.S. biennial budget is $94 million, of which the U.S.A. pays two-thirds, and the other twenty-three participating members [Cuba not counted] are supposed to pay the balance.)

Venezuela owed almost $800,000; Chile almost $700,000; Haiti, $435,000; Paraguay, $383,000; Bolivia, $381,000; Dominican Republic, $316,000; Uruguay, $250,000; Costa Rica, $216,000; El Salvador, $215,000; Ecuador, $128,000. In the report from the General Accounting Office, it was stated that Mexico was exporting "the same kinds of commodities that were being donated under the U.S. relief programs," and many other instances of U.S. aid failures in Latin America over the last decade were enumerated. Congressman Dante B. Fascell, Chairman of the House Inter-American Affairs Subcommittee, reported in May, 1971, that the Inter-American Development Bank had loaned more than $273 million to Mexico for irrigation projects "in areas where no crops can be grown, even with ample water."

The state, which is weak and which is aware of its shortcomings, develops a strong sense of xenophobia and chauvinism. The weaker the state, the stronger is the urge to invoke national pride among its citizens. Richard N. Adams wrote that "a constant stressing of American political stability is neither a convincing nor an ingratiating argument to offer Latins [1:278]. They are aware of this stability and would have imported it long ago if it were transferable." Adams continued, "The characteristically hierarchical, somewhat authoritarian and paternalistic patterns of Latin American governments need not be compared unfavorably with the more decentralized North American system." It should be recognized that this form is necessary to insure stability and to serve during the hiatus before literacy increases and a social conscience is created among the masses of the citizens. Adams might have called it "benevolent despotism."

The weaker the state, the greater is its attempt to establish a strong centralized government. It lacks confidence in the division of authority and responsibility. In states where *personalismo* is the order of the day, and each cacique sits with a Sword of Damocles over his head, no shrewd politico will permit the promotion of a subordinate to a position of equal or autonomous authority because that creates a rival for the seat of power. A real delegation of power can be made only in a strong state with a unified citizenry.

Between an inferiority complex and the problem of lack of a definitive identity and a perennial fear of unrest, most of the leaders of the Latin American nations have resolutely refused to face their national problems and to seek national remedies. The great Mexican philosopher and teacher, Antonio Caso, commented on the history of Mexico in *Apuntamientos de cultura patria* (Mexico, 1943):

> Our national problems have never been solved as they arose. . . . Mexico has proceeded cumulatively instead of following a uniform and graduated dialectical process. . . . Causes which existed prior to the Conquest and have become ingrained in us as well as others which arose later have joined to create great national problems that are so abstruse, diffi-cult and dramatic that we are filled with a hopeless despair. . . . We haven't solved the problem of democracy and now we are confronted with the great debate of socialism in its most acute and urgent form.

Even the philosopher Hegel is reported to have stated that the blindness of Latin Americans to their problems causes them to live "as an echo and reflection of the Old World, as its shadow and not as a reality." The fantasy of Latin American nationalistic thinking has evoked the belief among some of them that their hour has struck and that they are the possessors of "The Manifest Destiny" (54:81).

In international affairs, the Mexican President Venustiano Carranza on November 19, 1915, made a statement to which all Latin American nations still theoretically subscribe:

> The leading ideas in international policy are few, clear and simple. They come down to declaring that all countries are equal and must mutually and scrupulously respect their institutions, their laws and their sovereignties; that no country should in any form or for any motive meddle in the internal affairs of other countries; that no man should claim a better condition than that of citizens of the country where he goes to settle nor turn his status as a stranger into a title for exacting protection and privilege.

Among the reasons that Latin American nations either fear, feel inferior to, or have little respect for the United States are the following:

1. Although all of the Latin American nations, except Cuba and Panama, were independent by 1830 (Panama was created by Theodore Roosevelt in 1903 by imperialistically cutting it away from Colombia, and Cuba was liberated from Spain officially in 1902), none of the independent republics except Brazil and Mexico were regarded as of sufficient importance internationally to be invited to the first Hague Peace Conference held in 1899.

2. Constant reminders of history do not permit the people to forget the injustices of the colossus to the North against Cuba, Guatemala, Mexico, Colombia, Nicaragua, and Haiti. The dispatch of the U.S. Marines to Central American countries and Santo Domingo in this century and the policy of dollar diplomacy (the American flag was always there to protect our private investors regardless of the laws of the nations where the American capitalists sought their profits, a brand of diplomacy which is now abandoned) created resentments. These resentments remain to the present day. In addition, there are the C.I.A. activities such as the overthrow of Arbenz in Guatemala (he was a true communist) and the reports of the C.I.A. in Chile prior to and subsequent to the election of Allende.

3. Latin American politicians find American capitalism a convenient whipping boy. They use the names of American companies to arouse xenophobia among the masses and also as a means of diverting attention from their own malfeasance. Chileans use Anaconda Copper, Central American countries formerly used the United Fruit Co., Argentina and Peru condemn American and British oil companies; and Brazil attacks because we either "exploit" them, depress world prices on their coffee, or steal their land.

4. They find tremendous divergences between what we practice and what we preach.

The Monroe Doctrine was a unilateral declaration unsolicited by any of the then emerging Latin American nations. Although they did not oppose it and never publicly acknowledged it, they were grateful for it. However, its subsequent and consistent unilateral interpretation by Presidents Theodore Roosevelt and Woodrow Wilson showed that it was a weapon to serve our own ends, to impose our concepts. Wilson's statement that "we will teach them the meaning of democracy" was interpreted as an excuse to exploit them through our dollar diplomacy. That we have ceased these actions and that U. S. Marines do not bail out American entrepreneurs as we did formerly, have not erased the bitter memories of the incidents of this century.

The Latin Americans believe that we still use a dollar diplomacy, but of a different kind. Now, we buy support for our programs in organizations such as the O.A.S., by our grants-in-aid, soft loans, the Export-Import Bank, A.I.D. programs, Peace Corps personnel, and other official and semiofficial agencies disbursing our funds.

In some of the Latin American nations there appears to be an uncommonly large number of national holidays. These national holidays are observed with great fanfare and parades and speeches. What may seem an excessive number to sophisticated, self-reliant and confident nations, such as Britain, the United States, and even Spain, should be viewed as the desire of the governments to instill and arouse national identification and national pride in their citizenry.

In Mexico, there is a large and elaborate monument at the entrance to Chapultepec Park memorializing *Los Niños Héroes*, the Heroic Children. This refers to the young military cadets who allegedly leaped to suicide from the heights of Chapultepec rather than surrender to the American forces during the Mexican War of 1846-1848 (the U.S. name for the American invasion), or the American War (the name given to it by Mexicans). There are some who consider the suicide leap apocryphal, since they state that the Mexican daily press carried no account of any such acts of martyrdom, and that the first reports appeared almost thirty years later. One fact, however, has been confirmed. The evidence exists that the commander of the Mexican forces atop the hill had sent a request for reinforcements to General Santa Ana (of Alamo fame, and who was elected president of Mexico eleven times, but served only a total of four years). The Mexicans could have held out almost indefinitely if Santa Ana had fulfilled the request, but he was then engaged in some doubledealing and did nothing. The suicides, if indeed they occurred, resulted from the failure of their own supreme commander to act.

The annual speeches celebrating the suicide of *Los Niños Héroes* omit all such accounts of nonfeasance by the Mexican military leaders. Almost every town in Mexico has a street named Los Niños Héroes, as well as streets named for Madero, Juarez, and Cinco de Mayo, May 5th, 1862 (to celebrate the only real battle won by the Mexican Army against the invading French in 1863 at Puebla). All of these serve as reminders of the existence of the nation to its citizens.

Nationalism and xenophobia cannot be divorced from the need for *personalismo*. It is true that in times of stress and emergencies, all but the brave will seek refuge and protection. In like manner, Latin American nations, when faced with dilemmas for which no solution seems to exist, will drop all pretense of democracy and resort to a *lider máximo*, a caudillo.

The decade, 1950-1960, witnessed some momentous events in Latin American governmental history. One event is attributed directly to the American C.I.A.: the overthrow of the Jacobo Arbenz government of Guatemala, which had been branded as Communist. There was the overthrow of Perón in Argentina; Rojas Pinilla in Colombia; General Odría in Peru; Pérez Jiménez in Venezuela, and finally Batista in Cuba. All of these men had been dictators. All of these changes augured well for democracy in Latin America, at least we were so informed by our State Department and newspapers. A new day was dawning for all of Latin America, we believed. There is a French adage, *"La plus ça change, la plus c'est la même chose,"* "the more things change, the more they are the same." Now, 1975, we have a Communist dictator in Cuba, Castro; and unelected presidents in Argentina, Peru, Brazil, Bolivia, and Panama, all there by virtue of military coups. Sra. Peron came to the Argentine presidency because of the demise of her husband. She had been vice-president.

Where Communist parties operate legally, they are usually suppressed when martial law is imposed or when there is a suspension of constitutional liberties. When an American president is due on an official visit, the government may imprison Communist leaders three of four days prior to the arrival of the distinguished guest and release them after his departure. This action is not resorted to when other heads of state visit. Suppression and suspension of constitutional rights are the rights of the executive, and no one, except Communists, objects to the president's actions in imprisoning these people.

Every country has political parties. The Latin American parties differ in several respects from American parties. In the United States, each major party has a national committee, but these committees operate only on the national level and on national affairs. State committees, as well as those of the counties or municipalities, are autonomous. The fact is that the national committees are selected by the representatives of the smaller political units. Each level operates within its own sphere, although there are overlappings and power conflicts

between different levels. National platforms and pronouncements by national figures may be disregarded. This is
illustrated by the refusal of the southern states in the U.S.A.
to abide by the Democratic national party pledge of integration even ten years after the 1954 Supreme Court decision in
Brown vs. *Board of Education.*

This is the exact reverse of the operation of political
parties in almost all Hispano-American countries. There,
political parties are monolithic and the power at the top or
national level dictates local nominations and local patronage. While some independence of action may be exercised in
the national legislature, this independence is usually confined to vocalization and expression of opinion. When the
votes are counted, only the foolhardy dare to deviate, unless
the top man is losing his charisma or other support.
Whatever democracy of action exists, it is operational only
within the party conclaves.

The problem, or question, of federalism versus
centralism has not yet been determined or answered in most
countries. In Mexico, where PRI has dominated all elections
since 1920, chinks in the power structure are being noted
since 1968. Carlos Madrazo's untimely death, as well as that
of some of his followers, represents a setback to the efforts to
democratize PRI and to make the role of the president and the
"inner-family" less than that of absolute monarchs. In many
countries, the debate about, or antagonism to, centralism lies
dormant because governmental revenue comes from import
duties, excise levies, and national firms whose principal
offices and factories are close to the capital. Local land taxes
prior to 1960 were negligible and were used to pay provincial
and municipal salaries. As time progresses and the tax base is
broadened and enlarged (another vision of the Alliance for
Progress never realized) the local units of government will
perceive that there are additional sources of income within
their bailiwicks which might be used to enrich local coffers.

José Luis Romero, in *History of Argentine Political
Thought,* notes that the political groups in the interior of the

country are indifferent to the nation, *contra los porteños*, against those of Buenos Aires, and that they owe their allegiance to their *pequeña patria*, little country. This calls to mind Ramón Menendez Pidal's statement that the Spaniards feel responsible only to their *patria chica*, the village where they were born. This kind of allegiance will always favor federalism over centralism. Movements to urban areas will not change this political loyalty for at least one generation. Ties to the place of birth are not the only thing to be broken. The extended family ties must also be sundered or modified.

On January 22, 1966, the Brazilian Congress approved the new Federal Constitution which retained an emasculated legislature and vested all power in the executive. The president and his cabinet and appointees represent the power and the decision-making process of Brazil. The president rules by decree and the country is becoming heavily centralized. Ultimately, this will lead to another revolution. The states of Sao Paulo and Minas Gerais, which control the wealth and industry of Brazil, will continue to subscribe to this constitution only as long as the new president will do nothing to displease them. The reason for the growth of power in the executive is that inflation had been running uncontrolled for the previous ten years, and neither the legislature nor the previous president had been able to stop it. In Panama, the president paraphrased the well-known statement of Secretary of Defense Charles Wilson in 1954, "What is good for General Motors is good for the country." In Panama, what is good for the president is good for his country — take it or leave it.

As fulfillment of their desire to evidence national sovereignty, each Latin American nation operates an airline which drains its economy. Anatole France in his *Penguin Island* narrated a conversation of some ambassadors at a fictional diplomatic affair. One of the conversationalists represented a landlocked small country that was, no doubt, Switzerland. The ambassador stated that his country had the strongest navy in the world. One in the audience then said, "But, this is impossible. Everyone knows that your country has only one battleship, and its port is not even on your soil." To this the braggart replied, "You are correct. However, if we admit that we have only a third or fourth rate navy, it would be an admission that it is inferior, and therefore, incapable of engaging in battle, and, if it were so foolhardy to attempt battle, defeat would be total and speedy. Therefore, we either have to abandon a navy or keep it and boast vainly of its nonexistent importance."

At the present time, Mexico, Brazil, and Argentina are assembling and partially manufacturing automobiles. Most of them are American. The Latin American market can absorb the present production, but when expansion comes, as each country bends all efforts to such ends, the production will produce a glut on the market. The standard of living for more than 60 percent of their population must be increased tenfold before there will be sufficient purchasers. The products that bear American names do not have equal American quality, and cost twice that of those products made in the U.S.A., England, or Germany.

It is hoped that the Latin American Free Trade Association (LAFTA) will produce a version of the European Common Market with quotas assigned, and multiplication of senselessly competing industries obviated. This hope, however, has little to support its fulfillment. In an editorial (1970) in the *News* of Mexico City entitled, "If the Shoe Fits," the editor called upon Mexico to practice what it preaches "by easing, or even abolishing, tariffs on other Latin American goods." Mexico did not heed this appeal at the meeting of foreign ministers, and LAFTA exists more on paper than in practice.

The rise of Latin Nazis, as reported by UPI newsman Martin P. Houseman, in Chile, should come as no surprise to those conversant with the psyche of Latin Americans. The surprise that Nazism is now becoming obvious in Chile is hard to understand. In the better restaurants in Santiago, in the larger and more costly homes in Viña del Mar, Concepcion, and Santiago, one is likely to hear as much German as Spanish. There is evidence of transplanted aspects of German culture. For example, one of the popular table wines of Chile is the Riesling, a German type of white, dry wine. There is other superficial, as well as meaningful, evidence of the influence of German ideas. The Fuehrer for the Chilean Nazis is Franz Pfeiffer, who served a jail sentence for a fire bomb attempt on an Israeli fraternal club in Santiago. Chilean Nazis wear red armbands with black swastikas; they boast of their Western culture and their European white race, from which Jews and Negroes are excluded.

In *Nationalism and Communism in Chile,* Ernst Halprin wrote:

> In Latin America two countries with a considerably higher general living standard, better social conditions, a rather less inequitable distribution of wealth and an even more numerous and economically more powerful middle class than Chile, namely Argentina and Cuba, have been politically far less stable. This certainly disproves the widely held view that democratic stability is the natural result of general well-being and a strong middle class. [25:25]

Technically, "social dissolution" should be discussed under criminology. It is a crime in many Latin American states and has no identifiable counterpart in the United States. At times, it might be compared to a breach of peace, or contempt of court; and at other times to a violation of the Smith Act of the 1940s when we began our search for Communists and fellow-travelers or organizations which preached the overthrow of our government. Some illustrations may better clarify an understanding of this crime. Enactment of laws against "social dissolution" stems from nationalism and a desire to maintain the source of power and the status quo.

In 1962, the railroad workers of Mexico declared for a strike against the nationally owned railway. The Labor Court (also a court of conciliation and arbitration) declared such a strike illegal. The late David Alfaro Sequeiros, one of Mexico's three great muralists, and an acknowledged Communist, exhorted the railroad workers to go out on strike. Sequeiros was tried and convicted of the crime of social dissolution (agitating against the court's decree) and sentenced to seven years' imprisonment. President Adolfo Lopez Mateos pardoned him in 1964, just prior to the end of his presidential term of office. Sequeiros served about three years.

Newspaper editors in other countries are jailed because of the publication of stories, or rumors, considered inimical to the welfare of the state. Freedom of the press, as well as all other freedoms, is subservient, or subject, to the good and welfare of the state. King Louis' immortal words are to be recalled. He interrupted a judge who used the expression "the king and the state" to say, "I am the state." Napoleon also declared that he alone was the state.

Government by administrative agencies, even though some do exist, is unknown. However, there are certain semiofficial bodies which operate autonomously of all governmental supervision except that of the president. These bodies usually control oil production and processing, as in Argentina, Peru, and Mexico, and other national resources or services, such as the railway. Even though there is a board of directors operating the nationally owned electric light and power company in the Mexican Federal Government, it is only the president of the country who can raise the rates. Lopez Mateos quietly gave the company a 10 percent increase in the electric rates just before the end of his term in 1964. For three or four months thereafter, consumers, unaware of the rate change, complained bitterly about being overcharged; hours were spent contesting the bills, but never did any employees of the company refer to the presidential action. It was first mentioned in the newspapers three months after the event. The small item in the *Diario Oficial* had been overlooked.

Consumers had no voice in the matter, and no one dared criticize the decree because the time was too close to the former president's action, and criticism was not yet appropriate. Annual celebrations to observe the nationalization of the light company were held during the years of Lopez Mateos' term, even though there had been previous rate increases. The public was paying more, without improved service, than they did when American and British interests owned and operated the company at great profit and with large salaries.

Xenophobia is not only a dislike but also a fear of foreigners. It is a fear of what foreigners say about them that has moved some of our Hispanic-American neighbors to assume foolish positions. Once having moved themselves into a ludicrous position, they are hoist with their own petard and continue ignominiously, rather than lose face by admitting an error. The expulsion of an American reporter from Mexico in 1938 came about, it is said, because of his critical reports of the oil expropriation. The reporter was denied the right to reenter the country for almost twenty years thereafter. The *Children of Sanchez* by Oscar Lewis was almost suppressed because it cast "discredit" on phases of Mexican life and a segment of its society.

In the northwest of Mexico live the Tarahumara Indians. No one knows their exact number. They avoid civilization as if it were a plague and rarely come to the nearest village, which is on a principal Mexican highway. They speak their indigenous language and only a few know Spanish. They have opposed efforts of the government to aid them despite their poverty. Their standard of living is almost that of aborigines. They are not friendly even with other tribes of pure Indians who inhabit the general area almost contiguous to theirs. A few Jesuits and Franciscans have established contact with them and bring them some small amount of aid.

In the latter part of 1966, an over-zealous monk reported to an audience in Louisiana the pitiful conditions under which the Tarahumaras existed. The American sense of generosity was immediately kindled and ten carloads of foodstuffs were sent to lighten the blight under which the poor Indians lived. Unfortunately for all, the event was overpublicized. Great posters were placed on the sides of the railroad cars trumpeting to the world that the train of mercy was bringing gifts from the citizens of Lafayette, Louisiana, to the Tarahumaras. No one asked the Mexican authorities whether the cars of food could enter or for official papers of entry. No one asked the Tarahumaras whether they desired the food. No one asked anything. Charity, well-publicized, ruled the day. Everyone was expected to sing hosannas and paeans of praise and clear the tracks for the train of American generosity.

The Mexican government stopped the train at the border on the ground that import licenses were lacking. The government could have added that Mexico is a sovereign state, that it has a welfare department and an Indian affairs council, which has been attempting to aid the Tarahumara for many years. Last, but not least, Mexico has surplus food available for sale, most of which would have been more to the liking of the Indian recipients than that shipped from the States. Mexico is a proud nation and has good cause to be. It is a developing rather than an undeveloped country. Had there not been the attendant publicity and had the request been made in a quiet, orderly manner, the ten cars could have entered the country. Of course, how much would have found its way into the stomachs of the Tarahumaras is questionable. The publicity in the States reflected on Mexico and made it appear that it had ulterior motives for denying a permit and that it didn't care about the starving and dying Indians. Mexico felt that the well-publicized acts were humiliating to it because it might appear to many that the country could not, or would not, attend to the needs of its people.

Another ludicrous incident concerns Frank Sinatra. In 1965, the singer played the leading role in a moving picture which, I have been told, reveals that there is or was a divorce mill in the northern part of Mexico and that life in the border town is free and easy, morally speaking, and that standards are not of the kind which would meet the approval of Boston's Watch and Ward Society. Sinatra was barred from entering Mexico unless the scenes which reflected on the country were cut from the picture. It was not this action alone which highlights the paradoxical action of a nation which boasts of the freedoms which may be exercised in a democratic nation. Mr. Sinatra owns a home in Acapulco. The Mexican Constitution explicitly and unequivocally states that no foreigner may own any land within 100 kilometres (60 miles) of any border; i.e., the Pacific Ocean, the Gulf of Mexico, the United States, or Guatemala. (Most other Latin American nations have similar laws.) Elizabeth Taylor and Richard Burton own a home in Puerta Vallarta, and countless other foreigners own homes in Acapulco and other resorts on the coasts of Mexico. These facts appear in the press innumerable times each year. When notables of the screen or elsewhere acquire such sites, the fact is publicly proclaimed. (It may be that title is taken in the name of a Mexican lawyer or Mexican corporation, but this circumvention of the law is never stated. The law itself is evidence of xenophobia.)

Sinatra either refused, or could not cut the scenes, which may well have correctly represented conditions in Ciudad Juarez or other border towns. The Mexican Congress and officials castigated the state of Chihuahua several times during the years preceding 1966 because of the great number of divorces granted under the state's laws and of the mockery of the judicial process in this area of litigation. As one Mexican lawyer said, "You don't really have to appear, but if you want the proceedings to look good, you come in by train or plane at 9 A.M. and leave the country by 3 P.M. released from the bonds of matrimony." (Quickie divorces in Ciudad Juarez were finally halted at the end of 1970.)

Mexico has reason to be grateful to Sinatra. He not only contributed to its charities, but, in 1964, he put on one of his inimitable shows in Acapulco and raised many thousands of dollars for the poor and the orphans of Mexico and he did this without a fee. All very incongruous, si? But, this is Latin America, or at least in this instance, one country of Latin America.

Frank Tannenbaum, in the introduction to George

Wythe's *The United States and Inter-American Relations,*
wrote, "Latin American nations are sensitive, proud, suspi-
cious of our intent, dubious of our motives" (75:v). He
concludes that Dr. Wythe's thesis is that we cannot remake
Latin America and ought to stop trying. Dr. Tannenbaum
notes that this is a painful theme for American policy and
deserves careful examination. S. Y. Teng of Indiana University once wrote in a review of *America's Failure in China* that
the reasons for such failure "include the American political
tradition to view alien things in terms of an image of one's
self."

This thesis has been stated by many others in succinct
sentences such as, "American democracy is not exportable,"
and "Our way of life is American and need not, in fact, cannot
be imitated by others" for the reasons stated hereafter or
because of differences in values, basic goals, backgrounds,
historical experiences, needs, etc.

"Only the corrupt and the power-mad can find genuine
satisfaction in the contemplation of the history of Latin
American governments" (12:105). The problem in Latin
America is that liberals and reformers too often find themselves ultimately in common cause with their former oppo-
nents, the conservatives. Kalman H. Silvert raises the questions about a region which has proven that it has the
potential to industrialize, has created large and modern
cities, embraces social welfare programs, and "then proceeds
either to stagnate or to underdevelop" (12:107).

One of the lessons to be learned from Ibero-America is
that there are no simplistic answers or deterministic definitions for the complexities of society. *And, dollars are no
panacea.* Many Hispano-Americans are prone to measure
progress in economic terms and they ignore, or are insensitive to, the turtle pace of social development in education,
housing, clothing, shoes, and food.

Those who fail to identify with the secular national state
usually identify with social levels and the traditional patterns
of interclass mores and relationships. Most Latin American

governments are governments of men rather than governments of law. When the law is what men say it is at different times and *ad hominem* relationships are factors in such statements of law, then the principle of equality before the law has no significance.

As a footnote to this chapter, it should be pointed out that there was an error in the reports that referred to the reason for the Mexican expropriation of the properties of the American and British oil companies in 1939 as being "intense nationalism" (cf.17A:148). A dispute over wages had raged for several years between the foreign oil companies in Mexico and their employees. Litigation over the matter had gone to the Mexican Supreme Court several times. The decrees of the lower court to pay over 20 million dollars in back pay had been affirmed. The companies arrogantly refused to pay. The Mexican authorities, in an attempt to compromise, offered to have the employees accept a payment of 6 million dollars. The oil companies counteroffered with 4 million dollars and then became adamant.

The issues were then crystallized: who was to be the final authority in the country, and were the Mexican court decrees to be flaunted by foreign investors? The Mexican President Lazaro Cardenas had no choice except to assert his country's sovereignty. He reluctantly decreed expropriation. This was a legal step under the Mexican Constitution. The oil companies then offered to pay the 6 million dollars, but it came too late. For Cardenas to have reversed himself would have made Mexico a laughingstock among nations.

Mexico has completely repaid with interest the sums found to be due to all the companies for their properties.

12 ● Latin America and the United States

Most national groups in our country, as well as all the branches of our government, talk piously of social justice, egalitarianism, Christianity, and human relations, but, pragmatically, what evolves appears to be an admonition to others, "Do what I preach, not what I practice." The same dichotomy between our verbalizations and our deeds exists in all the groups and governments of Latin America. Why should their politicians be less greedy, less corrupt, their bureaucrats more lily-white, their leaders more idealistic, more altruistic, and less dictatorial than our politicians, bureaucrats and leaders?

We are practicing a great deception on ourselves rather than on the Latin Americans. They see the fraud of our pitiful protestations and they give us what we deserve: lip service and tongue-in-cheek promises in exchange for our dollars. They regard us as uncouth, if not as barbarians, and uncultured because we play a transparent role and are self-mesmerized into a state of taking our posture seriously. Sometimes our representatives in foreign countries, including ambassadors and high-level administrators of dollar-dispensing agencies, and our national executive on official trips abroad make rash promises and obligate our nation without having the necessary congressional commitments. The seeming warmth of official receptions abroad with government employees released from their duties and compelled to line the streets marking the route of our president into the capital of the host country and cheering according to cues and waving flags causes him to rise to the role of playing a grateful guest with reckless disregard for the taxpayers' money.

The Englishman, the Frenchman, the German, the Spaniard, Soviet Russia, and China carry on commercial relations with the twenty-odd Latin American republics. They make loans to them at going rates of interest. None of them impose sermons as the price of their aid and transactions. They treat the Hispanic American nations as sovereign states entitled to do as they please and err in their own ways. Only one demand is made by the Europeans, "Please pay your bills when due."

We issue press releases and resort to headlines to herald our efforts. When the AFL-CIO made a loan in 1964 to Mexico for the erection of the "Kennedy Housing Project" in Mexico City, press releases were sent to every newspaper in the United States, as well as in Latin America. The multimillion dollar loan was hailed as a great event because the working man of the United States was helping his ill-housed working colleagues south of the border to have suitable housing. Of course, this great humanitarian loan was to be repaid at 5½ percent interest. Of greater consequence was that the repayment of the loan was guaranteed by the Mexican government and by the U. S. Agency for International Development. There was no risk involved in the loan. The Mexican newspapers didn't print the last two facts, but everyone who was interested in the loan knew all the facts. Again, we fooled only ourselves. Furthermore, the subsequent scandal perpetrated by Mexicans in phases of the operation of the Kennedy project was not discussed in print but was bruited about openly in verbal form. The scandal was the doing of Mexicans, and the corruption was unknown to the AFL-CIO. However, the responsibility was in part attributed to America by some of those duped.

Much of the fiasco of the Alliance for Progress program was due to our failure to understand that too often in Latin America promises are equated with deeds. The promises of 1961 at Punte del Este made by the Latin Americans were not all made tongue-in-cheek. Undoubtedly, those who made them believed, at the moment of making them, that the promises would be fulfilled. Anyone can become starry-eyed when billions are glibly discussed and the vision of a better tomorrow can, as a mirage, be mistaken for reality. The cultural orientation of Latins is emotional and humanistic rather than mechanistic.

We never perceived the difference between Japan and Latin America in attaining democracy through industriali-zation. Japan succeeded because of "a tight autocratic control of the economy by a group of people who were determined to carry through with the industrialization process, and who were able to dictate and control the required measures" (Marston Bates, *Where Winter Never Comes*, 1952). Japan could suspend its democratic goals for the immediate goal of industrialization since Japan had the desire *and* the determi-nation to become a powerful nation in Southeast Asia. So often this kind of aggressive ambition is lacking in Hispano-America. With the increase in the price of oil, Venezuela now has this aggressive ambition. Our Latin neighbors place, properly, a high priority on education, at least verbally. Education has not solved the population explosion that plagues the countries. Costa Rica, with a 95 percent literacy, has a very high birthrate. One of the few great influences of the Church, aided and abetted by nonreligious tradition, is the imposition of obstacles to birth control. Latin tradition calls for a high reproduction and even Indian culture favors frequent pregnancies.

An integral part of the Alliance program was that "political freedom must accompany material progress." President Kennedy felt that political freedom could open the door to much needed reforms. The motto was, *Progreso sí! Tiránia no!"* So eager was Kennedy for action that he launched the program in advance of any Latin American commitment. Of course, with a promise of 20 billion dollars over a ten-year period, it was simple to secure approval for the alliance charter at Punte del Este on August 17, 1961. Ten ambitious goals were in the charter. It was not decided whether economic assistance or reform should come first. We wanted evidence of reform before aid but our neighbors wanted economic assistance first. The fiasco became evident in 1962 when the military of Argentina and Peru refused to accept the elections in their respective countries. By 1963 we had advanced one billion dollars but most was absorbed by "social overhead and bail-out funds."

Another meeting was held at Punta del Este in April 1967. This was a summit meeting of hemisphere presidents and Lyndon B. Johnson was among them. The presidents pledged "to give vigorous impetus to the Alliance for Progress." Nothing has happened in the intervening years.

The Latin American Common Market then envisioned to begin in 1970 has not passed into functioning reality. Pious words about improvements in education and raising rural standards of living and many scientific and technological programs have not produced any noticeable changes. The Latin American presidents promised to reduce military expenses but they have increased. With some slight oversimplification, the answer can be found in one word, "nationalism." There has been a marked growth in economic nationalism with an undertone of anti-Americanism. Solutions to problems are often found in radical political upheavals.

Latin Americans know that American leaders rarely reverse or abandon their policies. President Kennedy could not abandon the Alliance for Progress after a year or two because he and his aides had pointed to this as their major achievement. The chaos of Kennedy's domestic legislative programs could be pushed into the wings while the spotlight of the promise of a new future for Latin America occupied the stage. We underrate the political and diplomatic astuteness of our southern neighbors. They know us, our failings, our grossness, and our weaknesses better than we think. They capitalize on our foibles and will continue to make hay while we bask in the sun of self-imposed deception and gullibly swallow Latin American statistics.

Illustration of the acceptance of such figures is found in the continuous praise by U.S. officials of Mexico for allocating 25 percent of its budget to public education. In the first place, the record for the years prior to 1966 shows that expenditures for education never equaled stated budget allocations. (Again, the gap between promise and performance.) In the second place, Pablo Latapí, a Mexican who holds the doctorate in education, reveals in his book *Diagnostico Educativo Nacional* (34:123) that the 25 percent figure is false since it included monies which do not come from the federal government.

Furthermore, budgets in Latin America are manipulated by the executive branch of the government. Presidents can, and have, divert funds from one department to another. At best, the executive is bound only by the total amount of the budget. Specific allocations are, in essence, only tentative figures to be presented once and then forgotten until the following year. In Mexico, the Congress, which convenes only twice a week from September to December, receives the presidential budget on September 15 and must adopt it by December 15.

William Lytle Schurz noted that Latin Americans lack a sense of numerical precision so that the statistics of a nation "suffer from a general disregard of accuracy" (59:52). One of the most common phrases in Latin America is *más o menos*, more or less. This is used to qualify almost every statement of distance, time, money, or anything of mathematical or statistical content.

Henry Steele Commager and Richard B. Morris wrote in the introduction to Charles Gibson's *Spain in America*, "To the Latin American 'colonialism' and 'imperialism' too often serve as pejorative terms to explain their relationships to the people north of the Rio Grande" (20:ix). Americans fail to understand this underlying antipathy to them. Professor Emeritus Harry Stark, of the University of Miami, an old Latin American scholar, wrote in the *Miami Herald* (April 30, 1970), "that dislike for the United States is a tradition in Latin America . . . such dislike will continue, regardless what the U.S. does or does not do, as long as the United States remains the world's No. 1 nation . . . envy of the man higher up on the ladder is a deeply ingrained trait . . . maybe it is true that the Latin American nations, with strong military establishments, have been those most prone to replace constitutional government with dictatorships. But it is also true that . . . the army is often the only government agency sufficiently well-organized and disciplined to forestall chaos and maintain a semblance of law and order."

In too many of our relationships, we exhibit no knowledge of the fact that only Anglo-American tradition calls for the preservation of individual rights while in Latin America honor is more important than freedom. General Augusto Pinochet, head of the Chilean junta that overthrew Allende, and General Juan Velasco of Peru, with an identical rise to power, epitomize that Latin American disregard of the proverbial American freedoms and the rights of individuals.

One of the reasons advanced for the instability of Latin American governments is that the people had no experience in self-government prior to the acquisition of independence. Spain had been autocratic and permitted the New World residents to participate only to a limited extent in municipal affairs. The illiteracy of the mestizo and the slave-state of the Indian removed the vast majority from the slightest participation in government. Six Ecuadorian university students in the U.S.A., in 1970, attributed a lack of political stability in their own country in which reforms could be enacted. They labeled the Alliance a failure in Ecuador because of their government's bureaucracy and an absence of ample coordination with the U.S.A.

However, we must not overlook the European training and education of Simón Bolívar, José de San Martín, Bernardo O'Higgins, José Antonio de Sucre, Andres Bello and many others. Manuel Belgrano, Francisco Miranda, and others had the best education obtainable in the New World. These people had studied the French and the American Revolutions and were well-versed in the U.S. Constitution and the foremost French documents as well as the philosophy and writings of Locke, Mill, Rousseau, et al. All of the South American liberators were either suicides, were assassinated, or became expatriates. As Bolívar, who died at forty-seven, disillusioned and denigrated, wrote, "All who have served the Revolution have ploughed the sea."

Latin America was not ready for the republicanism that had been obtained through blood, and it is not ready for democracy now. Maybe the military of various countries are right when they say, "We are the conservers of constitutional government, and if the constitution does not work, we'll protect the people until a new constitution is written."

One of the results of a take-over by the military and the abolition of constitutional government is that the military ultimately regard their control of the government as perpetual. Undoubtedly Lord Acton's famous words, "Power corrupts and absolute power corrupts absolutely," come into play. Despite promises, Brazil's military have not relinquished control and General Juan Velasco in Peru and General Torres in Panama fail to exhibit any signs of restoring constitutional democratic government. That the military juntas are deaf to the voice of the people was the basis of a report by David F. Belknap of the *Los Angeles Times* of February 22, 1975. Despite six years of rule by Velasco and the enactment of some progressive and social reforms, the military regime has not won wide popular support. Belknap wrote that ". . . the Peruvian regime finds itself almost bereft of conscious support at home. No group is likely soon to displace or even seriously challenge the military, but the government encounters concerted opposition within many important sectors: labor, business, peasants, students, and professionals."

The February 1975 riots in Lima (called the *Limazo* riots) which resulted from the strike of the Lima police for higher pay and which were stifled by the national armed forces, revealed that the civilians, who were presumed to be in support of the ruling junta, did not exhibit any such support. The censorship of the press, the deterioration of many governmental services, such as the mail, have been eroding faith in the rule of the junta.

We mention, in passing, a slumbering Frankenstein whose awakening could lead to a heightening of antagonism to America, at the very least, or to the nationalizations of many American-owned industries, in addition to oil. The Frankenstein is a hydra-headed creature and may be known as "Grants and Loans." If there is a recession in the American economy, our Congress will undoubtedly slash grants to foreign countries. Regardless of the billions that we have poured into the coffers of other nations, each will say when "freeloading" is curtailed, "What have you done for me recently?" When we deprive them of further gifts, their sole concern will be the loss of funds to which they have become accustomed, and to which they feel that they have a legal right. Our affluence is theirs, at least to the extent that we have made them feel that we must share it with them; but our needs and those of our taxpayers are of no interest to them.

Repayment of loans and the interest thereon is facilitated by inflation and/or a growth in gross national product. If a nation's annual growth or increase in G.N.P. declines, or a recession occurs, repayment becomes a hardship or impossible. The following table covers all economic and military assistance and grants from 1946 to 1968. *The figures are in millions.* The table is taken from the "Special Report for the House on Foreign Affairs Committee" of May, 1969.

To the foregoing table should be added the millions of dollars that are poured into these countries by American foundations and by several other governmental subsidies.

| | REPAYMENTS INCLUDING | | | |
	LOANS	INTEREST	BALANCE	GRANTS
Argentina	722.4	440.7	281.7	94.6
Brazil	2,886.5	1,083.0	1,803.5	523.8
Chile	1,269.4	304.1	965.3	186.4
Colombia	812.3	259.4	552.9	167.0
Costa Rica	89.7	18.1	71.6	83.0
Cuba (to 1961)	37.5	8.3	29.2	4.0
Dominican Rep.	235.4	12.1	223.3	178.6
Ecuador	166.8	45.7	121.1	82.6
El Salvador	69.7	13.3	56.4	45.8
Guatemala	77.7	14.1	63.6	157.9
Haiti	33.9	10.8	23.1	77.5
Mexico	980.3	597.9	382.4	162.6
Nicaragua	105.9	19.0	86.9	56.1
Panama	133.8	25.8	108.0	92.6
Paraguay	62.1	18.5	43.6	46.3
Peru	440.6	265.3	175.3	149.5
Trinidad & Tobago (since 1953)	22.7	7.7	15.0	40.3
Uruguay	103.4	12.3	91.1	17.9
Venezuela	330.6	89.6	240.0	51.9

In addition to the foregoing, there are regional programs:

	LOANS	INTEREST	BALANCE	GRANTS
ROCAP (Central America)	85.4	1.6	83.8	25.1
Latin America Regional				1,542.0

We note without comment that Ecuador and Peru have unilaterally extended their national boundaries 200 miles into the Pacific Ocean and seize American (tuna) fishing vessels and impose fines ranging between $25,000 and $50,000. These fines are paid by the U. S. State Department. Ecuador has collected $54 million in fines over twenty years plus the confiscation of the fish. Brazil has done the same in the Atlantic, but this has been eased by agreement with our government.

Among the problems facing Latin America is that of bringing stability to the area. No attempt by the United States, no effort however vast, can be successful. The Chilean scholar Francisco José Moreno in his book, *Legitimacy and Stability in Latin America* (New York U. Press, 1969), states that the social traditions must be pursued to secure political stability, at least in Chile, and that instability is the inevitable price of nonconformity. He concludes that adoption of alien institutions leads to political instability which in turn hampers socioeconomic and political reforms.

In Latin American nations, political instability has been the rule and stability the exception for the past 150 years. It is difficult to establish any correlation between instability and the speed and degree of industrialization. Today, some countries are industrializing under conditions of relative stability while others are not. Instability cannot be blamed on Communist agitation. Other than Cuba, Chile is the only country in the area which legalized the Communist party almost twenty years ago. The party has consistently demon-strated considerable strength and the nation, until 1970, enjoyed stability and constitutional order. The 1970 election of Allende and the imposition of his Marxist theories, the setting of the lower economic classes against the rest of the country, the failure to take action against the illegal seizure of farmlands and other properties, and the lack of control of ruinous inflation, compelled the military forces finally to attempt to remove Allende from office. In the final moment, he committed suicide.

Another problem for American-type democracy is the same which besets several European nations and Israel. This is the multiplication of political parties. In Chile and a few other Latin American countries, some of these parties form a coalition—"front" is the most common word for such coalitions—prior to election time and then offer the electorate a potpourri of promises covering the spectrum from the right to the left but omitting the extremes of both sides. Of course, if elected, most of the promises are impossible of fulfillment because of the inability of any one party or front to secure a majority in both houses of a congress or because of the divergent political affiliations of the president and one or both houses of congress.

Election results from Latin American countries show that the urban masses are not radicalized. The word "Radical" as the name of a political party does not imply that it is radical in the sense that Americans understand the word. The Radical Party was formed in Chile in 1862. Initially it was the party of the northern mining capitalists and northern and southern federalists (Jay Kinsbrunner, *Chile: A Historical Interpretation,* Harper Torchbooks, 1973, p. 113). Later it became the most progressive of the leading parties. It opposed presidential authoritarianism and sought expanded suffrage rights, constitutional reforms, and church reforms. It was "radical" but not a democratic party. In the presidential election of 1946, Gabriel González Videla, a Radical, was elected by the Congress because he had not received a majority of the votes. Allende came to the presidency by the same route and for the same reason. "The multiparty nature of Chilean politics in the twentieth century and a president's dependence on more than one of them for power was demonstrated vividly in González's first cabinet. It was composed of three Radicals, three Liberals, and three Communists" (Kinsbrunner, *op. cit.,* p. 137). The president had to form a new cabinet after the resignation of the Liberal members and he formed a Radical cabinet. In 1948, he secured a law that made the Communist party illegal and it remained so until 1958.

Extremes of poverty and prosperity contribute to the fluctuation of election returns. But rarely do the urban masses seek the extremes of Communism, except in the election of Allende when inflation drove the masses to desperation. Usually, the extent of urban and rural unrest is exaggerated in the foreign press. Guerrilla warfare failed in Bolivia where a radical land reform had been carried out in the 1950s. In 1965 an even greater guerrilla effort failed quite as ignominiously in Peru, where there is real land hunger, and no such reform has taken place. General Velasco has nationalized some foreign business and used the confiscated wealth to throw bones to the impoverished.

It is not the stirrings of the masses that produce political instability in Latin America. On the contrary, political life in the area is characterized by the scarcity and short duration of mass movements. The explanation for the passivity of the Latin American masses lies in the basic inherited values held by the people which inhibit the development of collective action: individualism, fatalism, and paternalism, attitudes which lead people to expect political action to be taken and political benefits to be given from above.

In the essay "Bases of Political Alignment," in the book *New Approaches to Latin American History*, edited by Richard Graham and Peter H. Smith (University of Texas Press, 1974, p. 101) it is stated:

> Where the labor force is docile and easily manipulated, the regional elite is likely to be seigneural in social style and conservative in politics. The Indianoid peasant regions of central Mexico and the Colombian and Eduadorian highlands, as well as the slave-based societies of Popayán and Cartagena, provide examples of this pattern. Where the labor force became politically mobilized, the elite may have been forced to become liberal in posture and rhetoric in order not to lose control.

Political instability in Latin America is determined by the basic values of the peoples of the area. No injection of foreign capital, however substantial, and no amount of persuasion and diplomatic pressure, however persistent, can change such values in a hurry. If they do change in the course of time, there is no guarantee whatever that this change will be of a nature to ensure political stability and a democratic system!

As an instrument for ensuring democracy and stability,

the Alliance for Progress was therefore bound to fail. Examining its long-range aims, one finds that the Alliance is the modern version of an old American dream: that the happiness of other nations can be ensured by persuading them to adopt the triple formula of private enterprise, grass-roots democracy, and the family farm. This is ideology, not practical politics. It is a noble aspiration. It is not as ridiculous as was William Jennings Bryan's vision: "Our nation will lead the world in the great crusade which will drive intoxicating liquor from the globe." But it is no more realistic.

Actual U.S. policy in the area is almost based on such unrealistic aspirations. Patrick Holt, senior counsel to the U. S. Senate Committee on Latin America, said, "U.S. political policies have been dominated by short-range considerations." We all know what these considerations were: "There is a war on in Vietnam, so let us not have trouble elsewhere." Now, we have our own domestic problems. The results are either no policy or one of stop-gap measures to shore up existing governments, both democratic and dictatorial, provided they are reasonably friendly to the United States. We have been told by two who should know that our diplomacy is dated and that we lack a Latin American policy. Dr. Lloyd A. Free, director of the Institute for International Research of Princeton, testified before the House of Representatives subcommittee on International Organizations that "out of date diplomacy keeps the U.S. out of touch with the world," and that too many ambassadors regard diplomacy as it was practiced in pre–World War I days.

On August 3, 1971, Assistant Secretary of State for Latin America, Charles Meyer, conceded that we have no policy for Latin America. This frightening admission was made before the House Inter-American Affairs subcommittee. Mr. Meyer labeled the almost defunct Alliance for Progress schedule, "clearly unrealistic."

To aggravate the situation whereby we have "no policy," many Latins believe that our foreign policy is geared to control the economic destinies of Latin America. Albert O.

Herschman, professor of political economy at Harvard, advocated in January, 1970, that "U.S. firms should get out of Latin America." He advocated "selective liquidation" and relinquishment of control, not because they "willy-nilly" deplete the natural resources of America, *which they do not,* but because American corporations too often preempt the Latin entrepreneur. Our corporations are more alert and are willing to invest greater capital than the Latins. This has caused great resentment.

Even if we do not judge it by its distance from Alliance goals, the present U.S. policy of shoring up existing governments is ineffectual because many of these governments are so weak that no amount of shoring up will help. United States policy regards military coups against U.S.-backed democratic governments as deplorable but not catastrophic. The rationale of our State Department appears to be that the men who stage these coups are usually pro-American, on good terms with American businessmen and the Pentagon. Some, though by no means all of them, may eventually be persuaded to hand the reins back to a weak civilian government (a thing almost of the past). When there is a return to a weak civilian government, it lives in constant fear of the military losing patience with it. Peru, Bolivia, and Panama have now proven that they, as well as Brazil, have no intention of returning to impotent civilians or strong civilians who may turn dictatorial. Of course, when there are anti-Americans who come to power, as Allende or Arbenz, there is always the C.I.A. to aid in an overthrow. Mrs. Roberts of the Overseas Education Center of the League of Women Voters stated on February 15, 1975, that the C.I.A. co-opted the League's Overseas Education Center in Chile to aid wealthy Chilean women in their agitation of the masses to rise up against Allende.

A more serious view is taken of coups by civilians. Even if such a coup is not Communist-inspired, the fear exists that the Communists might end up in control. In such case, U.S. policy does not exclude the possibility of military intervention. Yet, such intervention would be a serious mistake.

Castro's stated aim for years has been to create several Viet-
nams in Latin America. His aims were spiked and he appears
to have turned to a more moderate course. Anyone familiar
with Communist tactics knows that his moderation does not
mean an abandonment of his original aim, and Russia would
not continue her support of Castro if she thought that he had
abandoned such aim.

Robert E. McNicoll, professor emeritus of Latin
American studies and a former member of one of our Latin
embassies, wrote in 1968,

> I trust that I do not reveal any secret when I say that there is
> no consistent policy at all among Foggy Bottom people. Deci-
> sions are made by many well-meaning individuals who proba-
> bly have not even read what their predecessors decided as little as
> five years before. . . . The Department of State has long oper-
> ated on a policy of having no policy, and decides each situation
> on an *ad hoc* basis so that no-one may be charged with originat-
> ing any policy.

Ex-President José Figueres of Guatemala testified before
a U.S. Congressional committee about the 1958 incidents
during the then Vice-President Nixon's Latin American trip.
Rotten eggs had been thrown at him and he had been spat
upon. Figueres said that people were expectorating, "not on a
person so much as on a policy."

There is a tacit assumption that once installed, a
Communist government could never be removed. This
implies another tacit assumption: that Soviet Russia would
tender massive military and economic aid to a second Cuba.
(The fall of Allende deflates such assumptions.) For without
Soviet aid such a government would be so weak that it could
easily be toppled or forced to change its policies. One need
only ask what would have happened to Castro if he had not
received Soviet military and economic aid from 1960 onward.
He would either be out of power, or he would be a very
different Castro with different policies. At the worst, he
would constitute a minor nuisance, like the former "Papa
Doc" Duvalier in Haiti. The only reason why Duvalier was

not a major problem to the United States is that he was not receiving Soviet arms.

The real problem facing the United States in Latin America is not insurgency, subversion, or political instability. The real problem is that of the Soviet presence. Is Russia a power of such unlimited economic resources that it would welcome a second Cuba? Is it a power of such boundless aggressiveness that it would go to war to enforce a right to send gunrunners to a second Cuba? The answer to both questions is obviously no, because in contrast to Russia's interest in Europe and Asia, its interests in Latin America are almost, but not absolutely, peripheral. Russia's failure in bolstering Allende when his toppling was apparent proves that Russian brinkmanship will never permit it to become militarily involved beyond its area.

To stop the very first Soviet block of gunrunners to another Cuba would not mean forcing a showdown. On the contrary, it would prevent a showdown. The 1962 missile crisis, which brought the world to the brink of nuclear war, occurred precisely because in 1960 the United States had failed to take the minor step of stopping the first gunrunners. Because of American permissiveness, small arms were followed by tanks and then inexorably by airplanes, artillery, and finally missiles. But Russia did not go to war over the missile issue, and would certainly not do so for the sake of delivering small arms to some other Latin American country. Russia practiced ably the "brinkmanship" which J. F. Dulles preached but practiced clumsily.

It might be argued that Russia could bolster up a second Cuba by purely economic means, without resorting to arms deliveries. The Soviets share at least one belief with Mao Tse Tung: that political power comes out of the barrel of a gun. In areas such as Latin America this dictum is completely true. Russia would not risk large-scale economic investment in a country where its position is so weak that it cannot even send arms. After the missile crisis had revealed the weakness of the Soviet position in Cuba, Castro had to scrap his ambitious industrialization plans because he could no longer get Soviet assurances of investment aid.

Summing up: insurgency, subversion, and political instability are unavoidable in Latin America. They would constitute a threat to the United States only in the unlikely event of leading to the establishment of a Communist regime supported by Soviet military and economic aid. Military intervention against such a regime might well produce the Latin American Vietnam which Castro had hoped to bring about. However, recent developments indicate that Castro is on the verge of being accepted by almost all of Latin America. The OAS embargo against him failed of being lifted in 1974 by only two votes. But it would be perfectly feasible to dissuade Russia from tendering military aid, not by public threats, but quietly, through diplomatic channels or the hot line. Or the question could be settled once and for all by an agreement of the OAS members to turn back gunrunners by joint intercep- tive action. Such an agreement might conceivably be easier to obtain than agreement to the unfortunate and ill-considered scheme of an Inter-American Intervention Force.

As for the Alliance for Progress, its unrealistic long-range aim should be replaced by some more modest and attainable goal, such as the spread of literacy or the extension of medical services to rural areas.

The United States could then afford to adopt a policy of strict nonintervention in the internal affairs of the Latin American republics. Such a policy would have salutary effects. One of the main impediments to progress in the area is the conviction of the Latin American elites that in the interest of its own security, the United States cannot afford the economic or political collapse of any of the republics. If only these elites would know that in the event of a collapse, the United States would restrict itself to the prevention of Soviet bloc gunrun- ning, and would neither bail them out financially nor inter- vene to save their persons and their property—then necessary reforms would certainly be speeded and saner economic policies adopted. The American taxpayer would thus save some money and the United States would be relieved of headaches over such problems as how to stop inflation in Brazil and how to distribute land in Chile.

We close with a naive statement that frightens diplomats. The time has come for our government to speak forthrightly and publicly about the shortcomings of the Latin governments. For Presidents Nixon or Ford to give an *abrazo* to Mexican Presidents Diaz Ordaz and Luis Echeverria and to call them Mexico's greatest may please the Mexican presidents, but masses of Mexicans who called Diaz a great disappointment (one of the kinder comments) regarded Nixon as a fool. Echeverria is plagued by guerrillas, kidnapings, and murders, which indicates that he is faced with growing discontent.

We should urge all our neighbors to the south to begin to set aside funds for the repayment of debts and to create sources for the payment of the inevitable nationalizations of many American firms in Latin America. We should not be faced at some future date with such claims as advanced by Chile and Peru that their examination of the American books going back twenty years reveal profits were greater than reported and therefore little or no money is due for the confiscation of the American property. We should cease guaranteeing American businesses which invest abroad.

To compliment, to use the carrot on a stick, are old ploys to win friends. However, when we are made to dance to the tune of Latins, when our government is reviled by every aspiring Latin politician, then we must use the Voice of America not to deride, not to belittle, not to sell a false image of ourselves of how much we are doing for them, but to help people realize that promises made to us have not been fulfilled and that they could have been. This can be done only by those who know the chinks in the armor of Latin Americans, who know of their Achilles heels and who know the culture of each of our Latin American neighbors.

Bibliography

1. Adams, Richard N., ed. *Social Changes in Latin America Today*. New York: Council of Foreign Relations, 1960.

2. Alba, Victor. *The Mexicans*. New York: Frederic A. Praeger, 1967.

3. Benitez, Fernando. *Los Primeros Mexicanos*. Mexico: Biblioteca Era, 1953. English translation under the name, *The Century After Cortes*. Chicago: Univ. of Chicago Press, 1965.

4. Benton, William A., and Stevenson, Adlai. *The Voice of Latin America*. New York: Harper & Bros., 1961.

5. Bonilla, Frank, and Glazer, Myron. *Student Politics in Chile*. New York: Basic Books, 1970.

6. Brandenburg, Frank. *The Making of Modern Mexico*. Englewood Cliffs, N.J.: Prentice-Hall, 1964.

7. Busey, James L. *Latin America: Political Institutions and Processes*. New York: Random House, 1964.

8. Chase, Stuart. *Mexico.* New York: Macmillan, 1931.

9. Clinton, Richard L. "APRA: An Appraisal." *Journal of Inter-American Studies* 12, no. 2 (April 1970): 296.

10. Clissold, Stephen. *Latin America: A Cultural Outline.* New York: Harper & Row, 1966.

11. Diaz Guerrero, Rogelio. *Estudios de Psicologia del Mexicano.* Mexico, D.F.: Antigua Libraria Robredo, 1961.

12. Form, William H., and Blum, Albert A. *Industrial Relations and Social Changes in Latin America.* Gainesville: University of Florida Press, 1965.

13. Encina, Francisco A. *Historia del Chile Desde la Prehistoria Hasta 1891.*

14. Filliol, Tomas Roberto. *Social Factors in Economic Development.* Cambridge, Mass.: M.I.T. Press, 1961.

15. Freyre, Gilberto. *New World in the Tropics.* New York: Vintage Books, 1959.

16. Ganivet, Angel F. *Idearium Espanol.* Madrid, 1905.

17. Gardner, C. Harvey. *Martin Lopez.* Lexington: University of Kentucky Press, 1955.

18. Gerassi, John. *The Great Fear in Latin America.* New York: Collier Books, 1968.

19. Geyer, Georgie Ann. *The New Latins.* New York: Doubleday, 1970.

20. Gibson, Charles. *Spain in America.* New York: Harper Torchbooks, 1966.

21. Gonzalez Pineda, Francisco. *El Mexicano.* Mexico D.F.: Editorial Pax-Mexicano, 1965.

22. Greer, Thomas V. "An Analysis of Mexican Literacy." *Journal of Inter-American Studies* 11, no. 3 (1969): 466.

23. Gruening, Ernst. *Mexico and Its Heritage.* New York: D. Appleton, 1928.

24. Hall, Edward T. *The Silent Language.* New York: Doubleday, 1959.

25. Halprin, Ernst. *Nationalism and Communism in Chile.* Cambridge, Mass: M.I.T. Press, 1965.

26. Henriquez Urena, Pedro. *A Concise History of Latin American Culture.* Translated by Gilbert Chase. New York: Frederick A. Praeger, 1966.

27. Herskovits, Melville J. *The Myth of the Negro Past.* Boston: Beacon Press, 1964.

28. Johnson, John J., ed., *Continuity and Change in Latin America.* Stanford, Cal.: Stanford University Press, 1964.

29. Johnson, John J. *Political Change in Latin America.* Stanford, Cal.: Stanford University Press, 1966.

30. Johnson, John J. *Simon Bolivar and Spanish American Independence.* New York: Van Nostrand, 1968.

31. Jorrin, Miguel. *Governments in Latin America.* New York: Van Nostrand, 1953.

32. Keen, Benjamin, ed. *Americans All: The Story of Our Latin American Neighbors.* New York: Dell Publishing Co., 1966.

33. Lambert, Jacques. *Latin America: Social Struggles and Political Institutions,* translated by Helen Ketel. Berkeley and Los Angeles: University of California Press, 1967.

34. Latapi, Pablo. *Diagnostico Educativo Nacional.* Mexico D.F.: Textos Universitarios, 1961.

35. Lipset, Seymour M., and Solari, Aldo, eds. *Elites in Latin America.* New York: Oxford University Press, 1967.

36. Lipset, Seymour M. *Revolution and Counter-Revolution.* New York: Basic Books, 1968.

37. Mackay, John. *The Other Spanish Christ.* New York: Macmillan Co., 1932.

38. Madariaga, Salvador de. *Englishman, Frenchman, and Spaniard.* London, 1929.

39. Madariaga, Salvador de. *Latin America Between the Eagle and the Bear.* New York: Frederick A. Praeger, 1962.

40. Madariaga, Salvador de. "Challenge in Latin America." *Saturday Review,* 25 March 1961, p. 14.

41. Madsen, William. *Christo-Paganism.* New Orleans: Middle Research Institute, Tulane University, 1957.

42. Martinez Estrada, Ezquiel. *Diferencias y Semejanzas Entre los Paises de la America Latina.* Mexico D.F.: UNAM, 1962.

43. Morner, Magnus. *Race Mixture in the History of Latin America.* Boston: Little, Brown, 1967.

44. Nehemkis, Peter. *Latin America: Myth and Reality.* New York: New American Library, 1966.

45. Northrup. F.S.C. *The Meeting of East and West.* New York: Macmillan, 1959.

45A. Olien, Michael D. *Latin Americans.* N. Y. Holt, Rinehart & Winston, 1973.

46. Payne, James L. *Patterns of Conflict in Colombia.* New Haven, Conn.: Yale University Press, 1968.

47. Paz, Octavio. *The Labyrinth of Solitude,* translated by Lysander Kemp. New York: Grove Press, 1961.

48. Petras, James. *Politics and Social Forces in Chilean Development.* Berkeley and Los Angeles: University of California Press, 1969.

49. Picon Salas, Mariano. *A Cultural History of Spanish America,* translated by Irving Leonard. Berkeley and Los Angeles: University of California Press, 1963.

50. Pike, Frederick B. *Chile and the U.S.* Notre Dame, Ind.: University of Notre Dame Press, 1967.

51. Pike, Frederick B. *Freedom and Reform in Latin*

America. Notre Dame, Indiana: University of Notre Dame Press, 1967.

52. Pike, Frederick B. *The Conflict Between Church and State in Latin America.* New York: Alfred A. Knopf, 1964.

53. Pike, Frederick B. "Church and State in Peru since 1840." *American Historical Review* 63, no. 1 (October 1967): 30.

54. Radler, D. H. *El Gringo.* Philadelphia: Chilton, 1962.

55. Ramos, Samuel. *Profile of Man and Culture in Latin America,* translated by Peter G. Earle. Austin: University of Texas Press, 1962.

56. Riesman, David, et al. *The Lonely Crowd.* New Haven, Conn.: Yale University Press, 1961.

57. Rycroft, Stanley. *Religion and Faith in Latin America.* Philadelphia: Westminster Press, 1958.

58. Sanchez, Luis Alberto. "The University in Latin America." *Americas,* Pan-American Union. Parts 1, 2, 3. Nov. 1961; Jan. and Feb. 1962.

59. Schurz, William Lytle. *Latin America.* New York: E. P. Dutton Co., 1964.

60. Shapiro, Samuel, ed. *Integration of Man and Society in Latin America.* Notre Dame, Ind.: University of Notre Dame Press, 1967.

61. Stabb, Martin S. *In Quest of Identity.* Chapel Hill: Universtiy of North Carolina Press, 1967.

62. Stoddard, Ellwyn R. "The U.S. Border as a Research Laboratory." *Journal of Inter-American Studies* 11, no. 3 (July 1968): 477.

63. Tannenbaum, Frank. *Ten Keys to Latin America.* New York: Vintage Books, 1966.

64. Urquidi, Victor L. *The Challenge of Development in Latin America.* New York: Frederick A. Praeger, 1965.

65. Veliz, Claudio, ed. *Obstacles to Change in Latin*

America. London: Oxford University Press, 1965.

66. Veliz, Claudio, ed. *The Politics of Conformity in Latin America.* London: Oxford University Press, 1967.

67. Verissimo, Erico. *Mexico.* New York: Orion Press, 1962.

68. Wagley, Charles. *The Latin American Tradition.* New York: Columbia University Press, 1968.

69. Wiarda, Ilda, and Wiarda, Howard J. "The Churches and Rapid Social Changes: Protestant and Catholic in Brazil. "*Journal of Church and State* 12, no. 1 (Winter 1970):13.

70. Wilkie, James W. *The Mexican Revolution.* Berkeley and Los Angeles: University of California Press, 1967.

71. Wilkie, James W. "Statistical Indicators of the Impact of National Revolution on the Catholic Church." *Journal of Church and State* 12, no. 1 (Winter 1970):89.

72. Wolf, Eric. *Sons of the Shaking Earth.* Chicago: University of Chicago Press, 1959.

73. Wood, James E., Jr. "The Rise and Growth of Religious Pluralism." *Journal of Church and State* 12, no. 1 (Winter 1970):1.

74. Worcester, Donald E. "The Spanish Past." *Journal of Inter-American Studies* 11, no. 1 (January 1969):66.

75. Wythe, George. *The United States and Inter-American Relations.* Gainesville: University of Florida Press, 1964.

76. Zea, Leopoldo. *The Latin American Mind,* translated by James H. Abbott and Lowell Dunham. Norman, Okla.: University of Oklahoma Press, 1963.

Index

AFL-CIO, 124, 166
A.I.D., 7, 17, 152, 166, 178
Alemán, Miguel, 95
Allende, Salvador, 71, 90, 102, 103, 115, 135, 151, 174
Alliance for Progress, 3, 7, 16, 17, 167, 168, 177
Anti-Semitism, 12, 107
APRA, 112, 115
Arcinegas, German, 11
Argentina, 3, 10, 12, 18, 26, 29, 34, 46, 66, 94, 95, 96, 126, 133
Aztec, 32, 52, 54, 65, 76, 98, 115, 117

Barbados, 18
Barriadas, 31
Benitez, Fernando, 39, 45, 104

Bolivar, Simon, 17, 31, 105, 170
Bolivia, 5, 13, 14, 17, 43, 84, 108, 115, 176
Brazil, 3, 10, 18, 22, 25, 29, 30, 34, 67, 69, 82, 94, 96, 156
Bullfighting, 40
Busey, James L., 43, 123

Cacique, caciquismo, 31, 94, 116, 117
C.A.C.M., 19
Carranza, Venustiano, 44
Castro, Fidel, 2, 20, 120, 134, 179, 180
Catholic, 60ff, 92, 102, 103, 115
Chapetones, 23, 31
Chile, 8, 10, 13, 14, 29, 71, 82, 94, 149, 174

Chinese, 47, 48
Cholo, 23, 36
C.I.A., 2, 151, 154
Colombia, 5, 7, 8, 9, 22, 23, 26, 46, 66, 69, 92, 108, 133, 135
Columbus Day, 36
Communism and communists, 108, 125, 130, 131, 133, 134, 136, 154
Costa Rica, 10, 26, 34, 66, 77, 82, 167
Cuba, 1, 2, 8, 12, 13, 17, 20, 27, 56, 63, 77, 120, 144, 148

Diaz, Porfirio, 44, 122
Diaz Guerrero, Rogelio, 28, 82
Diaz Ordaz, Gustavo, 133, 134, 182
Diego, Juan, 62

Echeverria A., Luis, 89, 95, 116, 122, 182
Ecuador, 5, 12, 13, 17, 72, 108, 173
El Salvador, 19, 115
English, 97, 104

Fascell, Dante B., 149
Frei Montalvo, Eduardo, 71
Favelas, 31
French, 43, 97, 104
Fuentes, Carlos, 35, 141

Ganivet, Angel F. de, 60
Gardiner, C. Harvey, 32
Gerassi, John, 2
German, 94, 97, 145, 158

Gibson, Charles, 60
Greer, Thomas V., 37
Gruening, Ernest, 1, 37, 54
Guianas, 18

Haiti, 17, 77, 148, 151
Henriquez Ureña, Pedro, 24
Herrera, Felipe, 4
Hidalgo y Costilla, Miguel, 1, 65, 106
Honduras, 13
Huerta, Victoriano, 4

Indian, 3, 4, 9, 11, 41, 46, 50, 53, 54, 62, 83, 104ff, 167
Inquisition, 25, 29, 53, 68, 80, 105, 147
Integration, 29, 34

Jamaica, 18, 47
Japanese, 48
Jesuits, 67, 128, 130
Jews, 12, 15, 25, 48, 68, 70, 74, 82, 94
Johnson, John J., 31, 37, 73, 94
Jorrin, Miguel, 120
Juarez, Benito, 1, 116

Kany, Charles, 24

Ladino, 22, 38
LAFTA, 157, 168
Lebanese, 48
Lipman, Aaron, 92
Lleras Restrepo, Carlos, 9, 135
Lopez Mateos, Adolfo, 95, 117, 133, 135, 159

Macho, machismo, 49ff, 73, 81
Mackay, John A., 63
Madariaga, Salvador de, 45, 128, 140
Madero, Francisco, 1, 43, 116, 121
Marshall Plan, 3
Martí, José, 1
Martínez Estrada, E., 47
Marxism, 69, 71. *See also* Communism
Maximillian, Emperor, 43
Mecham, J. Lloyd, 68
Mennonites, 48
Mestizo, 23, 36, 38, 46, 49ff, 61, 73, 76, 77, 84, 86, 97
Mexico, 1, 2, 3, 10, 11, 15, 17, 34, 35, 41, 42, 66, 69, 82, 93, 115, 116, 143, 150, 153, 158, 169
Miami Herald, 96, 149, 170
MNR, 115
Monroe Doctrine, 43, 152
Morrow, Dwight, 15

New Spain, 18, 70
Nicaragua, 18, 115, 151
Nigger, 22
Notario-publico, 22

OAS, 149, 152, 181
Oil, 167
Olien, Michael D., 47

PAN, 67
Panama, 10, 41, 84, 136, 144, 151, 156, 171
Paraguay, 18, 24, 96, 115
Paz, Octavio, 34, 38, 50, 142

Peace Corps, 152
Perez Jiménez, Marcos, 121, 154
Peron, Isabelle, 154
Peron, Juan, 72, 93, 121, 154
Peru, 10, 14, 17, 23, 31, 41, 69, 93, 171, 172, 173, 176
Pike, Frederick B., 92
Pincon Salas, Mariano, 7, 54
Pinochet, Agusto, 71, 91, 170
Platt Amendment, 20
Portugal, Portuguese, 18, 25, 26, 34
PRI, 67, 115, 118, 155
Protestant, 15, 69, 70, 73
Puerto Rico, 18, 19

Ramos, Samuel, 42, 52, 71
Rasco, José Ignacio, 7, 33
Reynal, Abbe, 52
Rojas Pinalla, Gustavo, 8, 9, 139, 154
Rycroft, Stanley, 25, 61

Sanchez, Luis Alberto, 37, 132
Schurz, William, 37, 77, 90
Segregation, 29
Sinatra, Frank, 161, 162
Spaniards and Spanish, 4, 45, 98, 104ff
Stoddard, E. R., 136
Summer Institute Linguistics, 26
Surinam, 13, 18
Syrians, 48

Tannenbaum, Frank, 10

Trade unions, 95, 96
Turcos, Turks, 48

UNESCO, 109
Uruguay, 10, 24, 34, 66, 84,
    94, 142

Vatican, 15, 72
Velasco, Juan, 90, 135, 170
Venezuela, 13, 18, 22, 31, 63,
    73, 94, 116, 133, 149, 167
Verissimo, E., 51

Villa, Pancho, 44
Vives, Luis, 68

Wagley, Charles, 4, 7
War of Cristeros, 14
Wilke, James J., 37
Wilson, Woodrow, 4

Zapata, Emiliano, 44, 121
Zea, Leopold, 33, 45, 107,
    140

DATE			